COO...
HEALTHY
&
FAST

Recipes & helpful hints
for cooks who say they don't have
time to cook healthy

BY RACHEL A. RUDEL
REGISTERED DIETITIAN

Fourth Edition, September 2006
Copyright 1994 by Rachel A. Rudel, RD, LRD,LD

This cookbook is a collection of favorite recipes, which
are not necessarily original recipes.

Published by: Apple A Day, Inc.
               213 Tenth Avenue West
               West Fargo, North Dakota 58078
               1-701-282-6826
               email: rachrudel@aol.com

ISBN: 0-9642510-0-0

Printed and manufactured in the United States of America
First Printing: 1994   8,000 copies

TABLE OF CONTENTS

DEDICATION

****

To my sons,
Mark and Paul

ACKNOWLEDGEMENTS

I thank my professional colleagues, friends and clients of the Red River Valley of the North for the support, suggestions, and wisdom preparing this recipe book.

My heartfelt gratitude to Dakota Pasta Growers, Carrington, North Dakota, and the North American Bison Cooperative, New Rockford, North Dakota.

A special thank you to my mother who nurtured and taught me the love of gardening, food, and cooking.

INTRODUCTION

In my work as a registered dietitian and educator, I am constantly confronted with the belief that healthy food cannot be delicious and fast to prepare. Today we generally prepare food on the run and eat frequently in fast food establishments.

In *Cooking Healthy & Fast*, my goal is to offer a resource to help people follow the recommended dietary guidelines using healthy recipes, and be able to prepare them quickly and with good taste!

Research indicates women want to spend thirty minutes or less selecting and preparing an evening meal. Men want to spend no more than fifteen minutes. How we have changed from the way Grandma spent hours preparing dinner!

My Favorite Recipes

Recipe	Page

MENU PLANNER

All menus include fat-free or skim milk

*North Dakota Chili
   Raw vegetable sticks
   Unsalted top saltine crackers

*Orange Pork Chops
   Fresh steamed broccoli

*Light Chick Wild Rice Soup
   French bread/soft tub margarine
   Non-fat yogurt

*Hamburger Cupcakes
   Glazed carrots
   Steamed rotini pasta

*Denver Tortilla Fold-ups
   Sliced fruits

*Crockpot Cheese and Potato Casserole
   Fresh vegetables and fresh fruit

*Salmon Cakes
   Baked potato
   Fresh fruit

*Zucchini Lasagna Casserole
   Sliced oranges

*Taco Casserole
   Thick and chunky salsa
   Raw vegetable sticks/fresh fruit

DIETARY GUIDELINES FOR HEALTHY AMERICAN ADULTS

*   Eat a variety of foods

*   Maintain a healthy weight and active lifestyle

*   Eat a diet low in fat, especially saturated fat

*   Limit sodium and sugar

*   Avoid alcohol, or drink in moderation

EAT A VARIETY OF FOODS

Over time, good nutrition has a profound effect on growth, development, long term health, and in general, quality of life.

The New USDA Food Guide Pyramid helps you choose a healthful diet that's right for you. Based on the DIETARY GUIDELINES, it offers practical nutrition advice for healthy Americans ages 2 years and over.

Each food group provides some, but not all, of the nutrients you need. No particular food group is more important than the other. To eat healthy, include all food groups.

The pyramid shape of the food guide illustrates that one should eat larger amounts of foods from the groups at the base (breads, cereals) - than from the groups at the top (fats, oils, sweets).

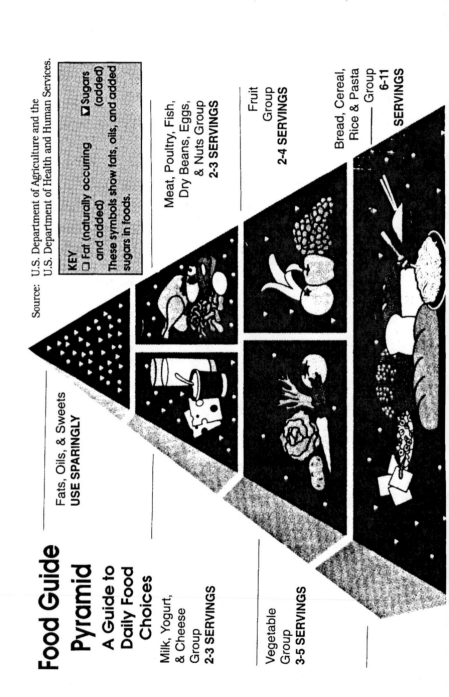

Food Guide Pyramid
A Guide to Daily Food Choices

Source: U.S. Department of Agriculture and the U.S. Department of Health and Human Services.

KEY
☐ Fat (naturally occurring and added)   ▼ Sugars (added)
These symbols show fats, oils, and added sugars in foods.

Fats, Oils, & Sweets
USE SPARINGLY

Milk, Yogurt, & Cheese Group
2-3 SERVINGS

Meat, Poultry, Fish, Dry Beans, Eggs, & Nuts Group
2-3 SERVINGS

Vegetable Group
3-5 SERVINGS

Fruit Group
2-4 SERVINGS

Bread, Cereal, Rice & Pasta Group
6-11 SERVINGS

WHAT COUNTS AS ONE SERVING?

FOOD GROUPS

Milk, Yogurt, and Cheese

1 cup of milk or yogurt	1 1-/2 ounces of natural cheese	2 ounces of process cheese

Meat, Poultry, Fish, Dry Beans, Eggs, and Nuts

2-3 ounces of cooked lean meat, poultry, or fish	1/2 cup of cooked dry beans, 1 egg or 2 tablespoons of peanut butter count as 1 ounce of lean meat

Vegetable

1 cup of raw leafy vegetables	1/2 cup of other vegetables cooked or chopped raw	3/4 cup of vegetable juice

Fruit

1 medium apple, banana, orange	1/2 cup of chopped, cooked, or canned fruit	3/4 cup of fruit juice

Bread, Cereal, Rice, and Pasta

1 slice of bread	1 ounce of ready-to-eat cereal	1/2 cup of cooked cereal, rice, or pasta

Source: U.S. Department of Agriculture and the U.S. Department of Health and Human Services.

How many servings do you need each day?

	Many women, older adults	Children, teen girls, active women, most men	teen boys, active men
Calorie level*	about 1,600	about 2,200	about 2,800
Bread Group Servings	6	9	11
Vegetable Group Servings	3	4	5
Fruit Group Servings	2	3	4
Milk Group Servings	2-3**	2-3**	2-3**
Meat Group Servings	2, for a total of 5 oz.	2, for a total of 6 oz.	3, for a total of 7 oz.
Total Fat (gram)	**53**	**73**	**93**

*These are the calorie levels if you choose low fat, lean foods from the 5 major food groups and use foods from the fats, oils and sweets group sparingly.

**Women who are pregnant or breastfeeding, teenagers, and young adults to age 24 need 3 servings.

Source: U.S. Department of Agriculture and the
               U.S. Department of Health and Human Services.

EAT A DIET LOW IN FAT, ESPECIALLY SATURATED FAT

Perhaps you know you need to cut down on the amount of fat you eat. A diet high in fat, especially animal fat, and cholesterol causes elevated blood cholesterol levels in most people. The elevated level is undesirable because it increases the risk of heart disease and stroke. It can also increase the risk of diabetes and possibly some cancers.

Recommended Grams of Fat and Saturated Fat at Various Calorie Levels

Calorie Level	Total Fat (30% of calories)	Saturated Fat (10% of calories)	Tsp. of Fat
1200	33-40 g	13 g	7-9
1500	42-50 g	17 g	9.5-11
2000	67 g	22 g	13-16
2400	66-80 g	25 g	15-18
3000	83-100 g	33 g	19-22

MAINTAIN HEALTHY WEIGHT

❤ * **Acknowledge** you want to maintain your present weight, or lose weight.

❤ * **Plan your meals**/snacks in advance so you have some idea of what you will eat and when you will eat.

❤ * **Make time** to eat breakfast.

❤ * **Eat like a King** for breakfast, a prince for lunch, and a pauper at night.

❤ * **Become educated** about Good Food Choices.

❤ * Seek out reliable nutrition education. A **registered dietitian** can give you reliable information.

❤ * **Don't go** for more than **6 hours** during the day **without food**.

❤ * **Limit portion sizes**. Measure foods. (A deck of cards is the same size as 3 ounces of meat.

❤ * **Include foods you enjoy** in your diet, don't try to live on rice cakes, diet pop and gummy bears.

❤ * **Eat something green** everyday: (Not green mint/ chocolate ice cream cones). Try broccoli!

❤ * Drink at least **8 cups of fluid everyday**. Water is the best!

❤ * Realize if you are really **thirsty, not hungry**.

❤ * Decide what you want to eat, **don't let other people influence your choices**.

❤ * **Keep** a daily **food diary**/record.

❤ * Eat **healthy** when you dine out. **Eliminate the extra fat and sodium**.

❤ * **Exercise** regularly (at least 3 x week).

❤ * Have an **occasional treat**.

ORGANIZING YOUR DAY... HOW MUCH FAT?

To Lower Cholesterol and Not Necessarily Lose Weight

✓   Normal Weight Women
          40-45 grams fat daily

✓   Normal Weight Men
          50-60 grams fat daily

To Promote Weight Loss:

✓   Women limit fat to 30-35 grams/daily

✓   Men limit fat to 45-50 grams/daily

BECOMING FAT SMART

#1 - TOTAL FAT:

A high fat diet can increase blood cholesterol. People do need <u>some</u> fat for good health, however, the average American diet contains about 37% fat. Obviously this is high, and should be <u>less</u> than 30% of total calories.

#2 - SATURATED FAT:

Saturated Fat can raise the level of cholesterol in a person's blood. <u>Sources of saturated fat</u> include: <u>butter, tropical oils (coconut, palm, palm kernal), animals fats, cream, whole milk, cheese made from whole milk, and ice cream.</u>
*Remember: Saturated Fats are Solid at Room Temperature.

#3 - UNSATURATED FAT:

Unsaturated fats include: polyunsaturated and monounsaturated fats.
Polyunsaturated fats include: Safflower, sunflower, corn, cottonseed, and soybean oils.
Monounsaturated fats include: olive, peanut and canola oils.
* Both types of oils are liquid at room temperature.
* Using unsaturated oils help lower blood cholesterol levels.
* Remember: All oils are high in fat and should be used in moderation. Other new unsaturated fats to experiment with are walnut, hazelnut and sesame oils.

A helpful hint: Use non-stick sprays when sauteing foods. Leave the butter or shortening at the grocery store!

#4 - HYDROGENATED FAT

The process of <u>hydrogenation, changes oils</u> from their <u>liquid state to a solid or semi solid state at</u> room temperature. These fats are <u>more</u> saturated than the original liquid oil. Examples are stick margarine, and shortenings. They are often found in bakery products, snack foods, and convenience mixes. When selecting margarine, the first ingredient should be liquid oil, not hydrogenated oil.

Hydrogenated vegetables are not better. Actually they are worse because they raise harmful cholesterol (LDL), and these fats lower food cholesterol (HDL).

These hydrogenated fats are called trans fats. The FDA is now working on the final rule which will require food manufacturers to list the amount of trans fat along with the saturated fat on the food label. The only way to determine if a food contains trans fat is to check for "hydrogenated" in the ingredient list, i.e. "partially hydrogenated vegetable oil."

COMPARISON OF DIETARY FATS

■ SATURATED FAT

POLYUNSATURATED FAT
- Linoleic Acid
- Alpha-Linolenic Acid (An Omega-3 Fatty Acid)

□ MONOUNSATURATED FAT

Fatty Acid content normalized to 100 percent

DIETARY FAT	CHOLESTEROL mg/Tbsp	Saturated Fat	Polyunsaturated Fat	Monounsaturated Fat
Canola Oil	0	6%	26% / 10%	58%
Safflower oil	0	9%	78% / Trace→	13%
Sunflower oil	0	11%	69%	20%
Corn oil	0	13%	61% / ←1%	25%
Olive oil	0	14%	8% ← 1%	77%
Soybean oil	0	15%	54% / 7%	24%
Peanut oil	0	18%	34%	48%
Cottonseed oil	0	27%	54%	19%
Lard	12	41%	11% / ←1%	47%
Palm oil	0	51%	10%	39%
Beef tallow	14	52%	3%→ / ←1%	44%
Butterfat	33	66%	2%→ / ←2%	30%
Coconut oil	0	92%	2%→	6%

WHERE'S THE
SATURATED FAT?

Food	Serving	Sat. fat g	Where
Prime rib	8 oz. slice	32	restaurants
Coconut milk	1/2 cup	21	tropical drinks
Dried coconut	1 oz.	16	topping, candy
Regular cheese	1 oz.	7	pizza, etc.
Ice cream	1/2 cup	7	dessert
Whole milk	1 cup	5	dairy goods
Chicken wings	4 ounces	4	restaurant

Source: *Bowes & Churches Food Values of Portions Commonly Used*

CHOOSE A DIET LOW IN FAT, SATURATED FAT, AND CHOLESTEROL

Simple ideas to help you cut down on total fat and saturated fat:

Choose Leaner Meats

• Remove visible fat from meat and poultry (the skin)

• Eat skinless white meat chicken and fish in place of high-fat red meats

Instead of	Try
Prime Rib	Flank, rump, London broil
Bologna, salami pastrami beef	Turkey, chicken tuna, lean roast
Barbequed ribs	Skinless barbequed chicken

BEEF

Type of Beef	Fat Grams Per 4 Ounce Serving
Beef Brisket (braised)	36.8
Ribeye Steak (roasted)	23.4
Rib Roast	36.8
Ground Beef (cooked)	24.6
Reduced Fat Ground Beef	4.0
Flank Steak (braised, lean and trimmed of fat)	15.7
Sirloin Steak (broiled)	20.9
T-Bone Steak (broiled)	27.9

FISH

Type of Fish	Fat Grams Per 4 Ounce Serving
Cod, Haddock, Lobster, Pollock, and Scallops	less than one
Chunk Light Tuna/Water	1.0
Flounder, Grouper, Pike, Snapper, and Sole	1.3
Monkfish, Ocean Perch, Rockfish, and Shrimp	1.7
Orange Roughy	8.0
Butterfish, Pacific Mackerel	8.9
Sockeye Salmon	9.7
Atlantic Herring	10.3
Chinook Salmon	12
Atlantic Mackerel, Pacific Herring	15.5
Sablefish	17.3

CHOOSE HEALTHIER COOKING METHODS

- Broil and bake with a rack so juices and fat fall away from meat

- Skim fat off meat juice before adding to gravies or stews

Instead of	Try
Frying	Roasting, baking, broiling, stir-frying, or grilling
Sauteing in butter or margarine	Sauteing with a small amount of oil or water
Cooking or baking with whole eggs	Egg whites or egg substitute

WATCH OUT FOR ADDED FAT

Now that you're choosing healthier foods and cooking them in healthier ways, don't undo your good work by adding high-fat sauces and condiments.

Instead of	Try
Butter/margarine	Jelly
Cream salad dressing	Homemade dressing with a small amount of oil or fat-free dressing
Gravy	Defatted meat juice
Regular mayonnaise	Mustard, low-fat mayonnaise

CHOOSE LOW-FAT DAIRY PRODUCTS

- Compare the fat contents on dairy labels

Instead of	Try
Whole or 2% milk	Skim or 1% milk
American or cheddar cheese (more than 5 grams of fat per oz.)	Low- or medium-fat cheeses like part-skim mozzarella (less than 5 grams of fat per oz.)
Sour cream	Nonfat or low-fat yogurt

TREAT YOURSELF TO HEALTHIER DESSERTS AND SNACKS

- Cakes, cookies, pies, and frozen dairy items should have less than 4 grams of fat per serving

Instead of	Try
Ice Cream	Ice milk, frozen yogurt, ice pops, sherbet
Potato chips, corn chips, nuts, or buttery popcorn	Pretzels or popcorn popped with a small amount of oil
Buttery, creamy, chocolate cookies	Fig bars, gingersnaps, graham crackers, vanilla wafers
Store-bought chocolate goods containing cocoa butter	Homemade chocolate goods with cocoa and oil

CHOOSE A DIET LOW IN FAT, SATURATED FAT, AND CHOLESTEROL

It is important to think about the <u>percentage of calories from fat.</u>

Calories are a source of energy for the body.

* 1 gram of carbohydrate has 4 calories
* 1 gram of protein has 4 calories
* 1 gram of fat has 9 calories
* 1 gram of alcohol has 7 calories

NOTE: (One gram is the weight of one paper clip.)

To understand this in terms of food, let's look at the following example:

Margarine   1 teaspoon =   5 grams of fat
(100% fat)

French Bread 1 slice =   15 grams carbohydrate
+ 2 grams protein
(0 % fat)

To Find % of Calories from Fat
Complete the Following Exercise:

1. Find grams of fat/serving. Multiply by 9.
   (9 calories per gram of fat.)
2. Find calories/serving.
3. Divide your total calories from fat by the total
   calories per serving.
4. Your answer is the % of calories from fat.
   Sample: 200 calories/one serving,
          has 6 grams of fat.
          6 grams fat x 9 = 54 calories from fat
          54 calories from fat ÷ 200 calories = 27%
          calories from fat.

CHOOSE A DIET LOW IN FAT

An Example of a Fat and Lean Dinner Menu

Big Fat Dinner
6 oz. prime rib
1 baked potato
1 teaspoon margarine
1/2 cup cauliflower with cheese sauce
1 cup fresh lettuce with 2 tablespoons blue cheese dressing
1 cup strawberries/mandarin oranges
1/2 cup chocolate ice cream

Total Calories: 987
Carbohydrates: 50 gm or 200 calories, 20% of total
Protein: 46 gm or 184 calories, 19% of total
Fat: 67 gm or 603 calories, 61% of total

My Lean Dinner
3 oz. sirloin
1 baked potato
1 tablespoon plain yogurt with garlic/chives for potato
1 cup steamed cauliflower with pepper
1 cup fresh lettuce with 1 tablespoon non-fat dressing
1 cup strawberries/mandarin oranges
1/2 cup ice milk

Total calories: 424
Carbohydrates: 55 g or 220 calories, 52% of total
Protein: 24 gm or 96 calories, 23% of total
Fat: 12 gm or 108 calories, 25% of total

Simple changes were made to reduce the amount of fat from 61% to 25%.

BIG FAT DINNER	MY LEAN DINNER
High fat prime rib	Low fat sirloin
6 oz. meat	3 oz. meat
margarine	non-fat yogurt
cheese sauce on cauliflower	pepper
blue cheese dressing	non-fat dressing
ice cream	ice milk

Recommendation:

Keep % of calories from fat at 30% or less. Percentage of calories from saturated fat at no more than 10%.

CHOOSE A DIET WITH PLENTY OF VEGETABLES, FRUITS AND GRAINS

- While most <u>fruits, vegetables,</u> and <u>grains</u> are <u>naturally low in fat</u>, there are a few exceptions: coconuts, olives and avocados

- Use <u>low-fat cooking methods</u> and watch out for added fat

- Fruits and vegetables are <u>rich</u> in <u>vitamins, miner- als, fiber,</u> and <u>water</u>

- <u>Use fruits for desserts</u> instead of high fat/sugar items

- A medium size <u>fresh apple contains no fat</u>, only 15 grams of carbohydrate and that equals 60 calories.

WHAT'S GOOD ABOUT FIBER

- High fiber foods help retain a feeling of fullness longer
- Reduces risk of possible colon and rectal cancer
- Certain types of fibers can reduce blood cholesterol levels
- Promote bowel regularity
- Stabilizes blood sugar in diabetics
- Improved absorption of minerals, (except calcium)

RECOMMENDED DAILY FIBER CONSUMPTION:

- 20-30 grams of mixed dietary fiber
- Whole grains, fruits, vegetables
- Drink at least a quart of water daily to avoid constipation when increasing fiber

FIBER CONTENT IN FOODS

Whole Wheat Bread	1 slice	1.4 grams fiber
White Bread	1 slice	0.4 grams fiber
All-Bran Cereal	1.3 cup	8.5 grams fiber
Cheerios Type Cereal	1 1/4 cup	1.1 grams fiber
Baked Beans with Tomato Sauce	1/2 cup	8.8 grams fiber
Apple with skin	1 medium	3.5 grams fiber

GOOD SOURCES OF FIBER

FRUITS, RAW

Apples	Oranges
Bananas	Pears
Blackberries	Raspberries
Blueberries	Strawberries

STARCHES

Beans (baked beans, kidney beans,
    pinto beans, navy beans)
Bran cereals
Bulgur (cracked wheat)
Dried peas (cooked)
Lentils (cooked)
Popcorn
While grain breads*
Whole grain cereals

VEGETABLES

Broccoli
Brussels sprouts
Carrots
Corn
Peas
Potatoes (with skin)
Pumpkin
Winter squash (acorn, butternut,
    hubbard)

*Look for whole grain or whole wheat as the first
ingredient. Some wheat breads, for example, are
brown in color because caramel coloring or molasses
is added, but refined flour that contains little fiber is
the main ingredient.

USE SALT AND SODIUM
ONLY IN MODERATION

> **Each recipe in this book includes**
> **sodium content per serving.**

WHAT ABOUT SALT/SODIUM?
* A compound made of 40 percent sodium and 60 percent chloride.
* Sodium is the main factor related to high blood pressure/hypertension along with family history, excess body weight, high alcohol consumption, and a high fat diet.
* Sodium helps maintain proper fluid balance in the body.
* Americans consume between 2,300-10,000 milligrams sodium each day.

SODIUM RECOMMENDATIONS
* Safe and adequate daily sodium range is 1100mg-3300mg daily (approximately 1 to 1 1/2 teaspoons of salt).

> **The American Heart Association recommends**
> **no more than 2,400 mg sodium per day**
> **for healthy adults.**

FOODS TO AVOID
* Table salt
* Packaged or processed foods - chips, salty crackers.
* High salt meats - smoked cured meats, ham, bacon, sausage, corned beef, hotdogs.
* Processed cheeses high in sodium.
* Seasonings and condiments - ketchup, relish, soy sauce, steak sauce and garlic and onion salt.

COOKING LOW SALT

* Omit and reduce salt from cooking and baking.

* Salt is really only necessary in yeast breads when baking.

* Use more herbs and spices.

SALT TO SODIUM CONVERSION

1 teaspoon salt = 2,300 milligrams sodium

1/2 teaspoon salt = 1,150 milligrams sodium

1/4 teaspoon salt =   600 milligrams sodium

1/8 teaspoon salt =   300 milligrams sodium

USE SUGAR IN MODERATION

SUGAR
- Provides simple carbohydrates
- Empty calories (no vitamins or minerals)
- Related to extra calories and weight gain

HOW TO RECOGNIZE SUGAR ON A LABEL
- **Look for:**
  maltose
  dextrose
  sucrose
  fructose
  lactose
  invert sugar
  brown sugar
  raw sugar
  confectioners sugar
  honey
  corn sweeteners
  corn syrup
  molasses

SUGAR CONTENT
- 1 teaspoon jam = 1 teaspoon sugar or syrup
- 1 ounce chocolate candy bar = 5 teaspoons sugar & 2 teaspoons fat
- 1/2 cup ice cream = 1/3 cup skim milk & 2 teaspoons fat & 3 teaspoons sugar
- 1 - 12 oz. can cola = 9 teaspoons sugar

SUGAR GUIDELINES

- Reduce sugar intake:

- In traditional recipes reduce the amount of sugar by 1/2 to 1/3.

- Avoid soft drinks, offer fresh fruits or ice water.

- Use spices such as cinnamon, nutmeg, and extracts such as vanilla, almond, peppermint, and chocolate extracts for that special taste.

- Avoid fruit "drinks". Use 100% fruit juice.

- Purchase fresh fruit for desserts or snacks. Avoid the candy bar, cookie and cake snacktime.

AVOID ALCOHOL, OR DRINK IN MODERATION

ALCOHOL FACTS

* Alcohol contains 7 calories per gram as compared to 4 calories per gram for carbohydrates or protein foods.

* Basically, alcohol contains "empty calories".

* When taken in excess, the body stores it as fat.

* Stimulates the appetite causing weight gain for many people

* Large amounts and chronic alcohol use damages the heart and other vital organs such as the liver and kidneys.

* Unborn babies are at risk with birth defects if a woman drinks heavily during pregnancy (Fetal Alcohol Syndrome (FAS)).

* Moderate use of alcohol is defined as no more than one drink per day for women and two drinks per day for men.

WHAT'S NEW ABOUT LABELING

1. ### Check for "Nutrition Facts"
   When the panel is titled "Nutrition Facts", it assures you that it meets the January 1993 Government Nutrition Labeling Requirements.

2. ### Check the Serving Size
   Foods that are alike now have the same, or standard serving sizes. This makes it easier to compare foods. They will be stated in household measures and reflect the amounts people actually eat. Always compare the label serving size with the amount you actually eat.

3. ### Check the Fat Grams
   How many fat grams are there per serving?

4. ### Check the Calories from Fat
   How many fat calories are you actually eating?

5. ### Check the Calories
   Calories still count - how many calories are there per serving and how many servings do you plan to eat?

6. ### Daily Values
   These are something new set by the government. Some are maximums for the day (such as 65 grams total fat or less if you eat 2000 calories/day); others are minimums (such as 300 grams total carbohydrate or more if you eat 2000 calories per day). The daily values for total fat, saturated fat, total carbohydrate, dietary and protein are based on the number of daily calories. However, daily values for sodium, potassium, vitamins and minerals stay the same no matter what the calorie level. The daily values for a 2000 and 2500 calorie diet must be listed on larger packages. Your own nu-

LABELING (Continued)

trient needs may be more or less than the daily values on the label. On a weight-loss diet these values generally are on the high end, so they will need to be adjusted to meet your needs.

7. **The % Daily Value**
   Here's the big change!
   % daily value shows how a food fits into an overall daily diet - they are based on a 2000 calorie intake. For example, is 13 grams of fat a lot or a little? Is 660 milligrams of sodium a lot or a little? You can use the % daily value as a guide to measure the nutrients in a specific food against your daily needs.

   a. If a food has 13 grams of fat and the % Daily Value is 20%, this means that 13 grams of fat is 20%, or 1/5 of the total daily fat recommended for a person who eats 2000 calories/day.

   b. If a food has 660 milligrams of sodium and the % Daily Value is 28%, this means that 660 milligrams of sodium is 28%, or about 1/3 of the suggested daily amount of sodium. Remember, the Daily Value for sodium is 2400 milligrams.

THE NEW LABEL

You can use % Daily Value to see what a serving of food contains compared to a 2,000 calorie reference diet. See the information below.

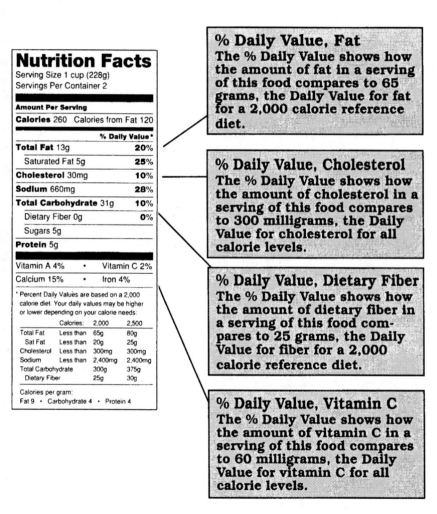

Nutrition Facts

Serving Size 1 cup (228g)
Servings Per Container 2

Amount Per Serving

Calories 260   Calories from Fat 120

	% Daily Value*
Total Fat 13g	20%
Saturated Fat 5g	25%
Cholesterol 30mg	10%
Sodium 660mg	28%
Total Carbohydrate 31g	10%
Dietary Fiber 0g	0%
Sugars 5g	
Protein 5g	

Vitamin A 4%	•	Vitamin C 2%
Calcium 15%	•	Iron 4%

* Percent Daily Values are based on a 2,000 calorie diet. Your daily values may be higher or lower depending on your calorie needs:

	Calories:	2,000	2,500
Total Fat	Less than	65g	80g
Sat Fat	Less than	20g	25g
Cholesterol	Less than	300mg	300mg
Sodium	Less than	2,400mg	2,400mg
Total Carbohydrate		300g	375g
Dietary Fiber		25g	30g

Calories per gram:
Fat 9 • Carbohydrate 4 • Protein 4

% Daily Value, Fat
The % Daily Value shows how the amount of fat in a serving of this food compares to 65 grams, the Daily Value for fat for a 2,000 calorie reference diet.

% Daily Value, Cholesterol
The % Daily Value shows how the amount of cholesterol in a serving of this food compares to 300 milligrams, the Daily Value for cholesterol for all calorie levels.

% Daily Value, Dietary Fiber
The % Daily Value shows how the amount of dietary fiber in a serving of this food compares to 25 grams, the Daily Value for fiber for a 2,000 calorie reference diet.

% Daily Value, Vitamin C
The % Daily Value shows how the amount of vitamin C in a serving of this food compares to 60 milligrams, the Daily Value for vitamin C for all calorie levels.

Source: U.S. Department of Agriculture and the U.S. Department of Health and Human Services.

WHAT ABOUT LABELING

YOUR LABEL DICTIONARY
New label terms can help you choose foods that are lower in calories, fat, cholesterol, and sodium, and high in fiber, vitamins and minerals. Here are some common label terms. ("Per serving" refers to reference amounts or standard servings set by the government.)

Key Words	What They Mean
Calorie Free	Fewer than 5 calories per serving
Light (Lite)	1/3 less calories or no more than 1/2 the fat of the higher-calorie, higher-fat version, or no more than 1/2 the sodium of the higher-sodium version.
Fat Free	Less than 0.5 gram of fat per serving
Low Fat	3 grams of fat (or less) per serving
Reduced or Less Fat	At least 25% less fat per serving than the higher-fat version
Lean	Less than 10 grams of fat, 4 grams of saturated fat and 95 milligrams of cholesterol per serving
Extra Lean	Less than 5 grams of fat, 2 grams of saturated fat, and 95 milligrams of cholesterol per serving
Low in Saturated Fat	1 gram saturated fat (or less) per serving and not more than 15% of calories from saturated fatty acids
Cholesterol Free	Less than 2 milligrams of cholesterol and 2 grams (or less) of saturated fat per serving
Low Cholesterol	20 milligrams of cholesterol (or less) and 2 grams of saturated fat (or less) per serving

MORE ABOUT LABELING

Key Words	What They Mean
Reduced Cholesterol	At least 25% less cholesterol than the higher-cholesterol version and 2 grams (or less) of saturated fat per serving
Sodium Free (No Sodium)	Less than 5 milligrams of sodium per serving, and no sodium chloride (NaCl) in ingredients
Very Low Sodium	35 milligrams of sodium (or less) per serving
Low Sodium	140 milligrams of sodium (or less) per serving
Reduced or Less Sodium	At least 25% less sodium per serving than the higher-sodium version
Sugar-Free	Less than 0.5 gram of sugar per serving
High Fiber	5 grams of fiber (or more) per serving
Good Source of Fiber	2.5 to 4.9 grams of fiber per serving

HEALTH CLAIMS
on the LABEL

To Make Health Claims About . . .	The Food Must Be . . .
Heart Disease and Fats	Low in fat, saturated fat and cholesterol
Heart Disease and Fruits, Vegetables and Grain Products	A fruit, vegetable or grain product low in fat, saturated fat and cholesterol that contains at least 0.6 gram soluble fiber per serving
Blood Pressure and Sodium	Low in sodium
Cancer and Fat	Low in fat or fat-free

Some other claims may appear on some labels.
These can be used only if a food meets specific
legal guidelines set by the government.

WHAT ARE IMITATION FOODS?

<u>**Imitation Foods**</u>

> Foods that do not meet the standard of identity for a particular product must be labeled imitation.

★ Imitation leaves a negative connotation.

★ Many cloned foods are extremely similar to the real food, but the FDA requires that foods that are nutritionally <u>inferior</u> to the original must be labelled imitation.

★ Nutritional inferiority is defined as a reduction of an essential vitamin, mineral or protein by 10% or more of the U.S. R.D.A. or in other words, 10% less than the real food of same nutrients. Fabricated foods are developed to be a cheaper product, and are put together from highly processed ingredients such as substitute meat burgers made from textured vegetable protein.

★ Imitation foods are not "junk foods", they simply do not supply 100% of the real thing.

★ One concern is that the vitamins and minerals found in the real foods are usually absorbed better by the body than the added nutrients found in cloned foods.

★ Real foods also contain essential trace nutrients that are not added to the imitations. Eg: Copper, selenium, chromium, manganese. We do not have exact requirements for these foods yet.

How do you spot an imposter? Read the ingredients.

The first ingredient in cheese is milk or cheese - not water.

Fruit juice should have the first ingredient listed as juice - not water.

Real meat will begin with meat - not soybeans or TVP (Texturized Vegetable Protein Products).

Some shellfish products use "surimi", a minced fish meat, most commonly Alaskan pollock. This product is blended with other ingredients such as crabmeat and flavoring. It contains little fat or cholesterol, but because it contains less niacin, potassium and protein, it must be labelled imitation crab.

TYPICAL INGREDIENT LABELS

Product	Ingredients
Orange Juice	100% orange juice concentrate
Imitation Orange Juice	Water, sugar syrup, corn syrup, orange pulp, citric acid, tripotassium phosphate, modified cornstarch, cottonseed oil, potassium citrate, tricalcium phosphate, vitamin C, natural and artificial flavors, sodium carboxymethylcellulose, xanthan gum, artificial color including FD&C yellow No. 5, thiamine hydrochloride (vitamin B1), BHA (preservative)
Mozzarella Cheese	Pasteurized whole or part-skim milk, cheese culture, salt, enzymes.
Imitation Mozzarella Cheese	Water, calcium, sodium caseinates (milk protein derivatives), partially hydrogenated vegetable oil (soybean and/or cottonseed oils), salt, calcium and sodium phosphates, artificial flavoring, adipic acid, sorbic acid (added as a preservative), artificial coloring, vitamin A palmitate, riboflavin

Food	Comments
Egg substitutes (made from egg whites and corn oil, with added vitamins, minerals, natural and artificial coloring)	Compared to the real thing, imitation eggs are substantially lower in calories, with no fat or cholesterol, but they're also slightly lower in protein and higher in sodium. A good alternative for people trying to cut dietary cholesterol.

FOOD EXCHANGES

Each recipe in this book includes exchange values.

Figures used to calculate the Exchanges are from the 1986 revised Exchange Lists for Meal Planning by the American Diabetes Association and American Dietetic Association.

The calories listed for each individual recipe are within 20 calories of the combined calorie value of the exchanges listed after each recipe. Also be aware that carbohydrates, proteins, calories, and fat used for each exchange list are averages and are not always the exact values for a specific food within the exchange list.

USING EXCHANGES

* To control total calories and fat by choosing foods from each food group.
* Specific portion sizes.
* Weight loss programs.
* Diabetic diets.

SIX FOOD GROUPS IN EXCHANGE SYSTEM

starch//bread
meat
vegetable
fruit
milk
fat

Free foods are foods with less than 20 calories per serving.

Combination foods are those that represent one or more exchange groups.

FOOD EXCHANGES

Many of the dessert recipes contain some sugar. If you are a diabetic using this recipe book, please check with your physician or registered dietician before using these recipes. Most people with diabetes can tolerate sugar within a mixed meal, but be aware of your individual meal plan.

BREAD/STARCH EXCHANGE
* Each serving 80 calories
* 15 grams carbohydrate
* 3 grams protein
* 0 grams fat

Several Food Examples:

Bread	1 slice
Graham crackers	3 squares
Popcorn	3 cups or 3/4 oz.
Shredded wheat cereal	1/2 cup

MEAT EXCHANGE
* Each serving 55 calories
* 0 grams carbohydrate
* 7 grams protein
* 3 grams fat

Several food examples:

Lean ground beef	1 oz.
Tuna in water	1/4 cup
Whole egg	1
Egg substitute	1/4 cup
95% fat free luncheon meat	1 oz.

Weigh meat after cooking.

VEGETABLES

VEGETABLE EXCHANGES
* each serving 25 calories
* 5 grams carbohydrate
* 2 grams protein
* 0 grams fat
* select 1/2 cup cooked or 1 cup raw

Several Food Examples:
Green beans
Broccoli
Tomatoes

FRUITS

FRUIT EXCHANGES
* Each serving 60 calories
* 15 grams carbohydrate
* 0 grams protein
* 0 grams fat

Several Food Examples:

Apple	1 medium
Banana	1/2 large
Strawberries	1 1/4 cup
Grapes	15
Dried fruit	1/4 cup
Orange juice	1/2 cup

MILK

MILK EXCHANGES

* Each serving 90 calories
* 12 grams carbohydrate
* 8 grams protein
* Less than 1 gram fat
  (skim, 1/2%, or 1%)   1 cup
* Dry nonfat milk   1/3 cup
    powder

FATS

FAT EXCHANGES

* Each serving has 45 calories
* 5 grams fat

Several Food Examples:

Margarine	1 teaspoon
Diet Margarine	1 teaspoon
Vegetable oil	1 teaspoon
Butter	1 teaspoon

CARBOHYDRATE COUNTING

Counting carbohydrates (starch, milk, fruit, vegetables, sweets) can help keep blood sugars (glucose) levels in a healthy range for people with **diabetes**.

* Spread carbohydrate intake throughout the day.

• Eat consistent amounts of carbohydrate at meals and snacks from day to day.

* Eat meals and planned snacks at regular times. Avoid skipping meals.

* Follow your food plan. A typical meal plan contains three-five carbohydrate choices for each meal, and one to two carbohydrate choices for each snack.

A carbohydrate choice has about 15 grams of carbohydrate.

* 1 choice   =   15 grams carbohydrate
* 2 choices =   30 grams carbohydrate
* 3 choices =   45 grams carbohydrate
* 4 choices =   60 grams carbohydrate

CONVERSION GUIDE

Total Carb Grams	Carb Choices
0-5	0
6-10	1/2
11-20	1
21-25	1 1/2
26-35	2
36-40	2 1/2
41-50	3
51-55	3 1/2
56-65	4
66-70	4 1/2

Stock up on HEALTH

ON THE CUPBOARD SHELVES
Breads: Whole wheat, French, pita, bagels, rolls, muffins.
Snacks: Crackers, pretzels, rice cakes, bread sticks
Cereals: Read-to-serve and hot
Pasta: Various shapes and sizes
Rice: Quick cooking brown and white
Baking mixes: Biscuit, pancake, corn bread, muffin, bread
crumbs
Potatoes: White and sweet
Onion & garlic
Beans: Dry, canned and instant
Canned foods: Fruits, vegetables, juices, water, chestnuts,
soup, tuna, chicken, turkey, evaporated
skim milk
Peanut butter
Sauces: Spaghetti, lite soy and teriyaki
Salad dressings: Light and fat-free
Vinegars: Cider, wine, flavored
Broth: Chicken, beef, vegetable
Oil: Cooking spray, canola, olive
Herbs & spices: The more the merrier
IN THE FRIDGE AND FREEZER
Tortillas and pizza crust
Toaster waffles
Pasta: Tortellini and ravioli
Fresh fruits in season
Vegetables: Carrots, peppers, celery, lettuce, broccoli,
cauliflower, green onions, ginger, mushrooms,
tomatoes
Frozen fruits, vegetables and juices
Dairy: Lowfat/skim milk, yogurt, shredded mozzarella,
string cheese, grated Parmesan, cottage cheese, light
sour cream
Eggs
Luncheon meats: Low-fat varieties
Meat: Lean ground beef, top round steak, pork loin strips
Poultry: Ground turkey, turkey cutlets, chicken breasts,
legs and thighs
Condiments: Mustard, ketchup, light mayo, salsa, pre-
chopped garlic
Margarine: Tub and stick

GROCERY STORE PRODUCTS: SHOP SMART

One must be thankful for all the excellent products developed for the low calorie, low fat, and low sodium consumer.

EGG SUBSTITUTE: each 8 oz. container is equivalent to 4 eggs.
Found in the frozen food section. One egg equivalent is 1/4 cup egg substitute.
Contains 25 calories, 0 fat, 0 cholesterol.

VEGETARIAN REFRIED BEANS: Lard has been replaced with soybean oil. Traditionally many brands still have lard. Check the label carefully.

SMOKED TURKEY SAUSAGE: Looks and really tastes like the real Polish sausage. It is lower in fat with only 2 grams, and 250 mg. of sodium. Limit this product as the sodium is still a bit high.

LIGHT PASTEURIZED PROCESS CREAM CHEESE PRODUCT: Comes in a tub. Use as regular cream cheese. Has half the fat with 5 grams/ounce and 160 mg of sodium.

FAT FREE PASTEURIZED CREAM CHEESE PRODUCT: Comes in a tub. Serving size is 2 Tbsp. with 30 calories and 0 grams of fat. Ideal for spreading on bagels, etc. Not suggested for baking. Does contain some sugar and 160 mg of sodium.

GROCERY STORE PRODUCTS

**FAT FREE
MAYONNAISE:** Blend this with small amount of mustard or vinegar if you think it is too bland for your taste buds.

YOGURT: (non-fat) Many are sweetened with sugar and some with Nutrasweet. Calories range from 80 to 150 for 6-8 oz. Try the plain and mix in your own favorite fruit. Non-fat yogurt (plain) can be used in place of sour cream.

**NON-STICK
COOKING SPRAY:** Great for frying lean meats, adding to vegetables, or spraying on your popcorn with your favorite spice flavor. A 1- to 2-second spray, contains 1 gram fat and no cholesterol, covers same cooking surface as one tablespoon of oil, which contains 15 grams of fat. Always spray cookware <u>before</u> heating it.

**FAT FREE RICE
AND CORN CAKES:** A lifesaver for something munchie. One caramel corn cake is 50 calories and 0 grams of fat, 5 grams of sugar and 7 grams of complex carbohydrates.

**FAT FREE
MARGARINE:** Nice for toast in the morning. The package directions indicate not to use this product for baking and frying. It has a high water content.

**NO-FAT
SOUR CREAM:** Looks and tastes like real sour cream. Regular sour cream has 6 grams of fat per 2 Tbsp. This product has 0 grams of fat. Check out the different brands, some taste more "real" than others.

GROCERY STORE PRODUCTS

**FROZEN ENTREES
(TV Dinners):**
Select those with less than 800 mg. of sodium, and fat limited to no more than 30% of the calories. Generally, they are 300 calories so the fat should be 10 grams or less. Wonderful for emergencies or if you cook often for one or two.

SPAGHETTI SAUCES:
Select a brand with 4 grams of fat/4 ounces. Good selections are fresh Italian, chunky garden style, and cheese.

CANOLA OIL:
Presently this oil has the least amount of saturated fat and the most amount of monosaturated fat. Canola is often blended with another oil, too.

CANNED SOUPS:
Several good brands are low in fat and sodium. Select brands with less than 30% of the calories from fat.

SOY SAUCE:
Purchase the regular one and dilute it with equal parts of water. Always check the sodium content of the lite or reduced version. The regular sauce diluted has 12 calories and 80 mg. sodium (1/4 tsp. with 1/4 tsp. water). Half tsp. of lite has 2 calories and 100 mg. of sodium.

GROUND TURKEY:
Search for the ones with 7% fat. Most of the frozen ground turkey has 15% fat which includes the skin ground in with the turkey meat. Ask your butcher for the fresh ground turkey without the skin at your local grocery meat department.

HELPFUL HINTS TO REDUCE YOUR TIME IN THE KITCHEN AND OTHER TIPS

1. Stock your freezer and cabinets with quick-to-fix staples such as canned or frozen vegetables, fish fillets, lean ground beef, boneless chicken breasts, pasta, and rice.

2. Check grocery stores and delis for presliced, diced, and prewashed fruit and vegetables from the produce section or salad bar. If this is the best way to include fresh vegetables in your diet, go for it!

3. Cook vegetables in the microwave.

4. Jot down menu ideas a week in advance. This is a game plan; make your plan and defrost meat in the refrigerator overnight.

5. Use dried onion instead of chopped fresh.

6. Use a salad spinner for cleaning lettuce quickly. Do a whole head of lettuce and store in the new vegetable plastic bags with the holes.

7. Double a recipe and freeze for future meals.

8. Keep a grocery list in a convenient place in your kitchen. Encourage your family to add to it when needed or when items look low.

9. To skin chicken parts, place a paper towel on the skin and pull.

AND OTHER TIPS

Apple Aberrations - For a different way to serve apples, try cutting them in half and spreading peanut butter on the cut half. Dip the peanut butter side into Rice Krispies. Kids love them!

No-Color Cauliflower - Add a small amount of lemon juice or vinegar to the water when cooking cauliflower. It maintains cauliflower's snow-white color.

Cheese Please - When grinding mozzarella or American cheese, sprinkle a bit of cornstarch among the layers to keep it from sticking together.

Pizza Slide - Spray your spatula with non-stick coating before serving pizzas to keep the slices from sticking to it.

Fresh Cottage Cheese - Turn cottage cheese upside down on shelf in refrigerator to keep it fresh longer.

Label Tip - Use two bags when packing leftovers for the freezer and put the description on masking tape on the inside bag (example: 100 slices ham). This prevents losing the label when rearranging freezer contents.

Sugar Softener - Cut an orange into eight sections and put skin side down in bag with hardened brown sugar to soften the sugar. Remove slices in five days or they may mold.

Better Meat Sauce - When preparing meat sauce, drain the grease from ground beef and rinse under hot water after it's browned and then add dry seasonings, mixing well before adding tomato products and water. This not only lowers the fat content of the final dish, but also prevents the dry seasonings from clumping together.

Rosy Applesauce - For an attractive dessert, add dry sugar-free red jello to applesauce to give it a rosy color. Add as much or as little as you would like for color and flavor.

Chocolate Chip Cookies - One cup of chocolate chips contains 915 calories. Half of calories come from fat, about 51 grams. Use only one-fourth cup chocolate chips, and you will have about 228 calories and 12.7 fat grams per recipe. Try the mini chocolate chips, that way every cookie will have some chips.

SAFE FOOD HANDLING
COLD STORAGE

These SHORT but safe time limits will help keep refrigerated food from spoiling or becoming dangerous to eat. These time limits will keep frozen food at top quality.

Product	Refrigerator (40°F)	Freezer (0°F)
Eggs		
Fresh, in shell	3 weeks	Don't freeze
Raw yolks, whites	2-4 days	1 year
Hardcooked	1 week	Don't freeze well
Liquid pasteurized eggs or		
egg substitutes, opened	3 days	Don't freeze
unopened	10 days	1 year
Mayonnaise, commercial		
Refrigerate after opening	2 months	Don't freeze
TV Dinners, Frozen Casseroles		
Keep frozen until ready to serve		3-4 months
Deli & Vacuum-Packed Products		
Store-prepared (or homemade) egg, chicken, tuna, ham, macaroni salads	3-5 days	These products don't freeze well
Pre-stuffed pork & lamb chops, chicken breasts stuffed with dressing	1 day	
Store-cooked convenience meals	1-2 days	
Commercial brand vacuum-packed dinners with USDA seal	2 weeks, unopened	
Soups & Stews		
Vegetable or meat-added	3-4 days	2-3 months
Hamburger, Ground & Stew Meats		
Hamburger & stew meats	1-2 days	3-4 months
Ground Turkey, veal, pork, lamb & mixtures of them	1-2 days	3-4 months
Hotdogs & Lunch Meats		
Hotdogs, opened package	1 week	
unopened package	2 weeks	In freezer wrap, 1-2 months
Lunch meats, opened	3-5 days	
unopened	2 weeks	

SAFE FOOD HANDLING (Continued)

Product	Refrigerator (40°F)	Freezer (0°F)
Bacon & Sausage		
Bacon	7 days	1 month
Sausage, raw from pork, beef, turkey	1-2 days	1-2 months
Smoked breakfast links, patties	7 days	1-2 months
Hard sausage - pepperoni, jerky sticks	2-3 weeks	1-2 months
Ham, Corned Beef		
Corned beef		Drained,
wrapped in pouch with pickling juices	5-7 days	1 month
Ham, canned		
Label says keep refrigerated	6-9 months	Don't freeze
Ham, fully cooked - whole	7 days	1-2 months
Ham, fully cooked - half	3-5 days	1-2 months
Ham, fully cooked - slices	3-4 days	1-2 months
Fresh Meat		
Steaks, beef	3-5 days	6-12 months
Chops, pork	3-5 days	4-6 months
Chops, lamb	3-5 days	6-9 months
Roasts, beef	3-5 days	6-12 months
Roasts, lamb	3-5 days	6-9 months
Roasts, pork & veal	3-5 days	4-6 months
Variety meats - Tongue, brain,		
kidneys, liver, heart, chitterlings	1-2 days	3-4 months
Meat Leftovers		
Cooked meat and meat dishes	3-4 days	2-3 months
Gravy and meat broth	1-2 days	2-3 months
Fresh Poultry		
Chicken or turkey, whole	1-2 days	1 year
Chicken or turkey pieces	1-2 days	9 months
Giblets	1-2 days	3-4 months
Cooked Poultry, Leftover		
Fried chicken	3-4 days	4 months
Cooked poultry dishes	3-4 days	4-6 months
Pieces, plain	3-4 days	4 months
Pieces covered with broth, gravy	1-2 days	6 months
Chicken nuggets, patties	1-2 days	1-3 months

COOKING TEMPERATURES

Product	Fahrenheit
Eggs & Egg Dishes	
Eggs	Cook until yolk & white are firm
Egg dishes	160
Ground Meat & Meat Mixtures	
Turkey, chicken	170
Veal, beef, lamb, pork	160
Fresh Beef	
Rare (some bacterial risk)	140
Medium	160
Well Done	170
Fresh Veal	
Medium	160
Well Done	170
Fresh Lamb	
Medium	160
Well Done	170
Fresh Pork	
Medium	160
Well Done	170
Poultry	
Chicken, whole	180
Turkey, whole	180
Poultry breasts, roasts	170
Poultry thighs, wings	Cook until juices run clear
Stuffing (cooked alone or in bird)	165
Duck & Goose	180
Ham	
Fresh (raw)	160
Pre-cooked (to reheat)	140

GETTING THE MOST NUTRITION FROM FOODS

When Shopping:
- Stock up on bread, pasta and potatoes, Relatively low in calories, they provide little or no fat.
- If buying fresh produce isn't practical, opt for frozen. It's the next best choice.
- Take advantage of fruits and vegetables in season. Know when they are available and plan recipes and menus around them to maximize nutrition.
- Choose dark green leaf lettuce over pale iceberg. The darker the color, the greater the beta-carotene content.
- Choose whole grain breads and cereals over refined ones. Not only do they provide more fiber, but they are also higher in vitamins and minerals.
- For a change, purchase protein foods that contain little or no saturated fat or cholesterol such as tofu, beans and dried peas.
- Keep plenty of fruit and vegetable juices on hand as an alternative to soft drinks. Fruit and vegetable juices are packed with vitamins. Soft drinks, on the other hand, provide little or no vitamins – only calories.
- Maximize the nutrient value and minimize the fat of desserts by choosing fresh fruits, ice milk or low-fat yogurts instead of rich cakes, cookies or ice creams.

When Storing:
- Keep milk and orange juice in paper or opaque containers. Direct light destroys B vitamins in milk and vitamin C in orange juice.
- Place fresh produce in covered containers and use as quickly as possible. Precious vitamins are lost during storage in the refrigerator.
- The same is true for the freezer. Cover and wrap foods tightly before storing in the freezer. Exposure to air accelerates nutrient loss. Be sure to use frozen foods within six to eight months of freezing for additional assurance against nutrient losses, especially vitamin C.
- Wait until just before serving to chop or dice fruits and vegetables for salads. Vitamin losses are minimized this way.

When Preparing:
- Maximize the nutritional value of vegetables by steaming, blanching or microwaving them. These cooking methods, rather than cooking in large amounts of water, save more vitamins from destruction.
- Plan to have an iron-containing non-meat food such as legumes, dried beans and peas along with good sources of vitamin C such as citrus fruits, cantaloupe or tomatoes. The vitamin C enhances the body's ability to absorb iron from the plant foods.
- Add non-fat dried milk to casseroles and sauces to get extra calcium without the fat of whole milk.
- Wrap baking potatoes in foil. They retain more vitamin C than when they are baked unwrapped.
- Use cooking water from vegetables to prepare soups and gravies. Vitamins and minerals that leech out into the cooking water are then recaptured. Or freeze the liquid in ice cube trays for later use.
- Make pasta, rice, vegetables and legumes the focus of meals instead of meat. Fat, cholesterol and calories in the meal drop and the nutrient and fiber content increases.

RECIPE MODIFICATIONS
FOR LOWERING
FAT AND REFINED CARBOHYDRATES

FOR.	TRY:
1 whole egg	1/4 cup egg substitute or 1 egg white and 1 tsp. vegetable oil or 2 egg whites
1 cup butter	1 cup margarine
1 cup shortening or lard	3/4 cup vegetable oil
1/2 cup shortening	1/3 cup vegetable oil
1 cup whole milk	1 cup skim milk
1 cup light cream	1 cup evaporated skim milk or 3 Tbsp. oil and skim milk to equal 1 cup
1 cup heavy cream	1 cup evaporated skim milk or 2/3 cup skim milk and 1/3 cup oil
1 cup sour cream	1 cup plain yogurt or 1 cup blenderized low fat cottage cheese (with lemon)
1 oz. regular cheese	1 oz. low calorie skim milk cheese
2 Tbsp. flour (as thickener)	1 Tbsp. cornstarch
1 Tbsp. salad dressing	1 Tbsp. low calorie salad dressing
1 oz. (1 square) baking chocolate	3 Tbsp. powdered cocoa and 1 Tbsp. oil
1 can condensed soup	Homemade skim milk white sauce (1 cup skim milk + 2 Tbsp. flour + 2 Tbsp. margarine)
Cream of celery soup	1 cup sauce + 1/4 cup chopped celery

For	Try

Cream of chicken .... 1-1/4 cup sauce
+ chicken bouillon

Cream of mushroom......................... 1 cup sauce
+ 1 can drained mushrooms

Cream cheese ....Blend 4 Tbsp. margarine
with 1 cup dry low fat cottage cheese.
Salt to taste; small amount of skim milk
is needed in blending.

1 oz. bacon (2 strips) ... 1 oz. lean Canadian bacon
or 1 oz. lean ham

1 cup all-purpose white flour............. 1 cup whole
wheat flour minus 2 Tbsp.; also, decrease the
amount of oil called for in the recipe by 1 Tbsp.
and increase the liquid called for by 1/2 Tbsp.;
or use 1/2 cup white + 1/2 cup whole
wheat flour; or use 3/4 cup white and
1/4 cup wheat germ and/or bran.

White rice .... Brown rice

Sugar .... Reduce amount. Reduction can be
up to 1/2 of the original amount. Use no more
than 1/4 cup of added sweetener (sugar, flour.

Fat .... Use no more than 1/2 Tbsp. of added
oil or fat per cup of flour; compensate
by increasing low fat moisture ingredient,
such as buttermilk, to add moistness.

Salt .... Reduce amount, try spices and herbs.

1 cup buttermilk or sour milk............. 1 cup skim
milk minus 1 Tbsp. milk; add 1 Tbsp. lemon
juice or vinegar. Let it stand 5-10 minutes
before adding to your recipe.

Oil ....In baking, substitute applesauce for oil,
such as cakes, muffins, etc.

HANDY CHART OF KITCHEN MATH WITH METRIC

KITCHEN MATH WITH METRIC TABLES

Measure	Equivalent	Metric (ML)	
1 Tbsp.	3 tsp.	14.8	milliliters
2 Tbsp.	1 oz.	29.6	milliliters
1 jigger	1-1/2 oz.	44.4	milliliters
1/4 cup	4 Tbsp.	59.2	milliliters
1/3 cup	5 Tbsp. + 1 tsp.	78.9	milliliters
1/2 cup	8 Tbsp.	118.4	milliliters
1 cup	16 Tbsp.	236.8	milliliters
1 pint	2 cups	473.6	milliliters
1 quart	4 cups	947.2	milliliters
1 liter	4 cups + 3-1/2 Tbsp.	1,000.0	milliliters
1 oz. (dry)	2 Tbsp.	28.35	grams
1 lb.	16 oz.	453.59	grams
2.21 pounds	35.3 oz.	1.00	kilogram

THE APPROXIMATE CONVERSION FACTORS FOR UNITS OF VOLUME

To Convert from	To	Multiply by
teaspoons (tsp.)	milliliters (ml)	5
tablespoons (Tbsp.)	milliliters (ml)	15
fluid ounces (fl. oz.)	milliliters (ml)	30
cups (c.)	liters (l)	0.24
pints (pt.)	liters (l)	0.47
quarts (qt.)	liters (l)	0.95
gallons (gal.)	liters (l)	3.8
cubic feet (ft³)	cubic meters (m³)	0.03
cubic yards (yd³)	cubic meters (m³)	0.76
milliliters (ml)	fluid ounces (fl. oz.)	0.03
liters (l)	pints (pt.)	2.1
liters (l)	quarts (qt.)	1.06
liters (l)	gallons (gal.)	0.26
cubic meters (m³)	cubic feet (ft³)	35
cubic meters (m³)	cubic yards (yd³)	1.3

SIMPLIFIED MEASURES

dash = less than 1/8 teaspoon
3 tsp. = 1 Tbsp.
16 Tbsp. = 1 cup
1 cup = 1/2 pt.
2 cups = 1 pt.

2 pt. (4 c.) = 1 qt.
4 qt. (liquid) = 1 gal.
8 qt. (solid) = 1 peck
4 pecks = 1 bushel
16 oz. = 1 lb.

If you want to measure part-cups by the table-spoon, remember:

4 Tbsp. = 1/4 cup
5-1/3 Tbsp. = 1/3 cup
8 Tbsp. = 1/2 cup

10-2/3 Tbsp. = 2/3 cup
12 Tbsp. - 3/4 cup
14 Tbsp. = 7/8 cup

CONTENTS OF CANS

Of the different sizes of cans used by commercial canners, the most common are:

Size	Average Contents
8 oz.	1 cup
picnic	1-1/4 cups
No. 300	1-3/4 cups
No. 1 tall	2 cups
No. 303	2 cups
No. 2	2-1/2 cups
No. 2-1/2	3-1/2 cups
No. 3	4 cups
No. 10	12 to 13 cups

Appetizers, Dips, Dressings & Seasonings

CHEDDAR CHEESE BALL

1 cup non-fat cottage cheese
4 oz. light cheddar cheese
   (label says part-skim)
1 Tbsp. chopped pimiento
1-1/2 tsp. minced onion
1/2 tsp. Worcestershire sauce
1/8 tsp. cayenne
2 Tbsp. chopped fresh parsley

Blenderize cottage cheese until smooth. Grate cheddar cheese. Combine all ingredients except parsley in a medium-size bowl. Chill in the freezer for 30 minutes and then form mixture into a ball. Roll in parsley and serve on a plate with low-fat wheat crackers.

Yield: .... 8 (1/4 cup) servings
Calories: 55
Fat: .... 2 g
Cholesterol: .... 9 mg
Sodium: .... 244 mg
   (To reduce sodium,
     use low-sodium cheese.)
Dietary Exchanges:.... 1/2 Fat
                    1/2 Skim Milk
Preparation Time: ...... 50 minutes

SPICY GUACAMOLE WITH TORTILLA CRISPS

1 avocado, seeded, peeled and cut up
1/2 cup nonfat yogurt
2 Tbsp. light mayonnaise
1/4 tsp. garlic powder
1/4 tsp. salt
1/4 tsp. cayenne

Tortilla Crisps:
4 (6 inch) flour tortillas
Nonstick cooking spray
2 tsp. chili powder

Peel avocado, cut up, and place in a blender with other ingredients. Blend smooth. Chill. Spray tortillas with nonstick cooking spray, and sprinkle with chili powder. Broil for 3 minutes. Cut into triangles and serve with guacamole dip.

Yield:	8 (2 Tbsp.) servings
Calories:	110 (2 Tbsp. dip + 1/2 tortilla)
Fat:	6 g
Cholesterol:	less than 1 mg
Sodium:	140 mg
Dietary Exchanges:....	1 Fat
	1 Vegetable
	1 Bread/Starch
Preparation Time:	30 minutes

CHRISTMAS TREE CANAPES

3 oz. reduced-calorie cream cheese
2 Tbsp. catsup
1 Tbsp. horseradish
1/4 tsp. garlic powder
1 dash cayenne
1/4 cup chopped fresh parsley
6 oz. imitation crab, thawed and flaked
8 slices white bread

Using a Christmas tree cookie cutter, cut a Christmas tree shape out of each slice of bread. Reserve shapes and discard edges. Mix all ingredients into softened reduced-calorie cream cheese. Spread this mixture evenly over slices of bread. Place under preheated broiler until lightly browned. Serve immediately.

Yield: .... 8 slices
Calories per slice: 116
Fat: .... 3 g
Cholesterol: .... 14 mg
Sodium: .... 365 mg
Dietary Exchanges:.... 1 Bread/Starch
1/2 Lean Meat
Preparation Time: ...... 15 minutes

MOCK SOUR CREAM

*This is great on baked potatoes
or as a dip for vegetables.*

    1/4 cup skim milk
    1 cup low fat cottage cheese

Place all ingredients in blender and mix on high speed until smooth and creamy. Add seasonings, such as dill, to add flavor if this is being used as a dip.

Yield:	12 (2 Tbsp.) servings
Calories:	15
Fat:	Trace
Cholesterol:	1 mg
Sodium:	81 mg
Dietary Exchanges:	1/3 Lean Meat

SMOKED SALMON SPREAD

1 tub (12 oz.) light cream cheese product
1/2 cup light sour cream
1 tsp. Liquid Smoke
1 Tbsp. lemon juice
1-1/2 tsp. Worcestershire sauce
1/8 tsp. salt (optional)
1/8 tsp. pepper
1 can (15-1/2 oz.) red salmon, drained,
 or 2 cups cooked and flaked fresh salmon
2 Tbsp. chopped celery
2 Tbsp. chopped green onion

Have cream cheese at room temperature. Remove skin from salmon and mash bones. Blend first seven ingredients in a mixer. Stir in salmon, celery and onion.

Variation: Liquid Smoke may be omitted.

Yield:	24 (2 Tbsp.) servings
Calories:	65
Fat:	4 g
Cholesterol:	20 mg
Sodium:	157 mg
Dietary Exchanges:....	1/2 Lean Meat
	1 Fat

CREAMY SEAFOOD DIP

4 oz. light cream cheese product
   (1/3 of 12 oz. tub)
1 pt. low fat cottage cheese
3 Tbsp. lemon juice
2 tsp. prepared horseradish
1/4 tsp. Tabasco sauce
1/4 cup chopped green onions
1 can (6-1/2 oz.) minced clams,
   shrimp, or crab, drained

Have cream cheese at room temperature. In blender or food processor, blend cheeses and next three ingredients until smooth. Stir in onions and seafood. Serve with raw vegetables or crackers.

Variation: Add 1 tsp. Liquid Smoke when blending ingredients.

Yield: .... 24 (2 Tbsp.) servings
Calories: 30
Fat: .... 1 g
Cholesterol: .... 6 mg
Sodium: .... 1 mg
Dietary Exchanges:.... 1/2 Lean Meat

FRESH APPLE-RAISIN DIP

1 med. apple, cored, cut into chunks
2 Tbsp. orange juice
2 Tbsp. slivered almonds
1 Tbsp. raisins
1/2 tsp. cinnamon
1/2 tsp. lemon juice
Celery sticks, gingersnap cookies
   or graham crackers

In food processor bowl with metal blade, combine all ingredients except celery sticks. Process with 10 to 12 on/off pulses until mixture is coarsely chopped. Serve with celery sticks. Store in refrigerator.

Yield: .... 16 (1 Tbsp.) servings
Calories: 20
Fat: .... 1 g
Cholesterol: .... 0 mg
Sodium: .... 35 mg
Dietary Exchanges:.... Free

PINEAPPLE ALMOND FRUIT DIP

1 (8 oz.) container (tub) light pasteurized
   process cream cheese product
3/4 cup drained crushed pineapple
   in its own juice
1 Tbsp. brown sugar
1/2 tsp. almond extract

In blender container or food processor bowl with
metal blade, combine cream cheese product and
pineapple; blend until well mixed. Add brown sugar
and almond extract; blend well. Serve at once or cover
and refrigerate until serving time.

Yield:	24 (1 Tbsp.) servings
Calories:	25
Protein:	1 g
Carbohydrate:	2 g
Fat:	2 g
Cholesterol:	3 mg
Sodium:	55 mg
Dietary Exchanges:	Free

SPICY YOGURT FOR FRUIT

    1 cup low-fat vanilla yogurt
    1/4 tsp. ground cinnamon
    1/8 tsp. ground cardamon or nutmeg

In small bowl, combine yogurt, cinnamon and cardamon or nutmeg. Chill. Just before serving, add dressing to fruit and toss well.

One Serving:	1 Tbsp.
Calories:	12
Fat:	0.2 g
Cholesterol:	1 mg
Sodium:	9 mg
Dietary Exchanges:	Free

SPINACH DIP

1 pkg. (10 oz.) frozen chopped spinach
1/4 pkg. (2 Tbsp.) dry vegetable soup mix
1-3/4 cups plain nonfat yogurt
1/4 cup reduced calorie mayonnaise
1 can (8 oz.) water chestnuts,
    drained and chopped
2 Tbsp. chopped green onions
1/4 tsp. dry mustard

Thaw spinach, drain and squeeze until dry. Stir dry soup before measuring to mix evenly. Mix all ingredients. Chill and serve with raw vegetables or slices of French or sour dough bread.

Yield: .... 14 (1/4 cup) servings
Calories: 40
Fat: .... 1.50 g
Cholesterol: .... 4 mg
Sodium: .... 93 mg
Dietary Exchanges:.... 1 Vegetable

HOMESTYLE
SALAD DRESSING

1 cup plain low-fat yogurt
1 Tbsp. Dijon mustard
1 tsp. dill weed
1 tsp. sugar

Blend together yogurt, mustard, dill weed and sugar.
Refrigerate until ready to use.

Yield: .... 16 (1 Tbsp.) servings
Calories: 10
Fat: .... 0.1 g
Cholesterol: .... 0 mg
Sodium: .... 39 mg
Dietary Exchanges: .... Free

TOMATO DRESSING

2 ripe tomatoes, chopped
1 stalk celery, finely chopped
1 carrot, grated
1/2 red pepper, diced
1/2 green pepper, diced
1/4 cup scallions
1/2 tsp. garlic powder
1/4 cup red wine vinegar
2 Tbsp. olive oil

Combine all ingredients. Store in covered container in the refrigerator. Stir before serving. This keeps well for 3 days. This dressing is great on pasta or fresh green salads.

Yield: .... 10 (1/4 cup) servings
Calories: 12
Fat: .... 0 g
Cholesterol: .... 0 mg
Sodium: .... 118 mg
Dietary Exchanges:.... 1/2 Vegetable
Preparation Time: ...... 15 minutes

TOTE-ALONG DRESSING

    1 can (12 oz.) low-sodium tomato juice
    3 Tbsp. fresh lemon juice
    1 Tbsp. finely chopped onion
    1 Tbsp. minced fresh parsley
    1-1/2 tsp. arrowroot powder
    3/4 tsp. granulated sugar
    1/4 tsp. garlic powder
    1/8 tsp. salt
    1/8 tsp. ground black pepper

Combine all ingredients in screw-top jar; shake to blend. Pour into small saucepan and cook over medium heat, stirring. Bring to a boil and continue cooking, stirring, 1-2 minutes or until slightly thickened. Allow to cool. Return to jar and keep refrigerated.

Yield:	20 (1 Tbsp.) servings
Calories:	4
Fat:	.02 g
Cholesterol:	0 mg
Sodium:	15 mg
Dietary Exchanges:....	Free

Rita Stutzinger
Dakota Medical Center

DESSERT SPICE BLEND

Use in cakes and cookies or to sprinkle on toast

>   2 tsp. ground cinnamon
>   2 tsp. ground nutmeg
>   1 tsp. ground ginger
>   1/2 tsp. ground allspice
>   1/2 tsp. ground cardamon
>   1/4 tsp. ground cloves

Mix ingredients together and store in shaker bottle for toast. Substitute mixture for spices in your favorite cookie or cake recipe.

Yield: .... About 1/3 cup
Calories: 0

HERB BLEND FOR BEEF

    1 Tbsp. dried marjoram
    1 Tbsp. dried basil
    1 Tbsp. dried parsley
    1 Tbsp. dried celery leaves
    1/4 tsp. dried summer savory
    1/4 tsp whole thyme

Crush dried herbs and blend thoroughly. Sprinkle on beef during cooking or use in a shaker at the table. Store extra in a tightly-covered glass container.

SEASONING BLEND

4 Tbsp. citric acid
2 Tbsp. parsley flakes, crushed
2 Tbsp. black pepper
2 Tbsp. paprika
1 Tbsp. garlic powder
1 Tbsp. ginger powder
1 Tbsp. onion powder

Mix together. Use in shaker on table. Store extra in tightly covered glass container.

Yield: .... About 3/4 cup
Calories: 0

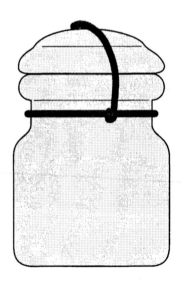

SHAKE AND MAKE FOR FISH & POULTRY

2/3 cup non-fat dry milk powder
1/2 tsp. pepper
1/2 tsp. dry mustard
2 tsp. paprika
2 tsp. low-sodium, chicken-flavored
    bouillon granules
1/2 tsp. poultry seasoning

Mix all ingredients thoroughly. Moisten meat slightly and shake in mixture. (If using chicken, remove the skin first.)

Bake according to recipe.

Yield: About 2/3 cup, enough for one chicken or
    several fish fillets.

SPICE BLEND FOR FISH

　　1 Tbsp. dried basil
　　1 Tbsp. dried chervil
　　1 Tbsp. dried marjoram
　　1 Tbsp. parsley flakes
　　1 Tbsp. dried tarragon

Crush dried herbs and blend thoroughly. Sprinkle on fish during cooking or use in shaker on table. Store extra in tightly covered glass container.

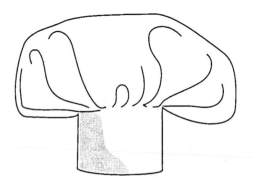

Beef
&
Pork

CABBAGE HAMBURGER CASSEROLE

4 cups roughly chopped cabbage
1 lb. very lean ground beef,
    brown with 1 small onion
Dash oregano and pepper
3 cups fresh tomatoes, chopped or
    1 #303 can reduced salt stewed tomatoes
    (optional: 1 sm. can no-salt added
    tomato sauce)

Brown very lean ground beef, brown with small onion. Rinse meat in colanders under hot water to reduce fat. Season meat with a dash of oregano and black pepper. Preheat oven to 350°. Layer roughly chopped cabbage, very lean ground beef and top with tomatoes in a 2 quart casserole sprayed with non-stick spray. Bake at 350° F for 45-60 minutes.

Yield: .... 6 servings
Calories: 233
Fat: .... 14 g
Cholesterol: .... 65 mg
Sodium: .... 73 mg
Dietary Exchanges:..... 1 Vegetable
                          2 Medium-Fat Meat
                          1 Fat

Joyce & Tom Pettinger

BAKED MEATBALLS

2 lbs. extra lean ground beef (9% fat or
   less) or ground turkey (7% fat)
1/2 cup egg substitute (equal to 2 eggs)
1 Tbsp. dried parsley
1 cup oatmeal or cracker meal or oat bran
1 cup skim milk
1 tsp. salt (optional)
1/2 tsp. ground pepper
2 tsp. onion powder
1/4 tsp. nutmeg

Preheat oven to 425°. Mix all ingredients. Shape into
1-1/2 inch balls. Arrange on two baking sheets that
have been sprayed with non-stick coating. Bake for
12 minutes or until done.

Yield:	About 48 meatballs
	16 (3 meatball) servings
Calories:	135 (beef)
	125 (turkey)
Fat:	7 g
Cholesterol:	35 mg
Sodium:	47 mg
Dietary Exchanges:.....	1/4 Starch
	1-1/2 Medium Fat Meat

GROUND BEEF-HASH BROWN BURGERS

1 lb. lean (80%) ground beef
1 cup frozen shredded hash-brown
    potatoes, thawed, coarsely chopped
1 tsp. Worcestershire sauce
1/2 tsp. seasoned salt
1/2 tsp. onion powder
1/4 tsp. pepper

In large bowl, combine all ingredients; mix lightly until well blended. Shape mixture into six 3/8-inch-thick patties. Place on broiler pan; broil 4 to 6 inches from heat for 8 to 10 minutes or until of desired doneness, turning once. Or, place on grill rack; cook on gas grill over medium heat or on charcoal grill over medium coals for 8 to 10 minutes or until of desired doneness, turning once.

Yield:	6 burgers
Calories:	200
Fat:	13 g
Cholesterol:	47 mg
Sodium:	190 mg
Dietary Exchanges:	1/2 Starch
	2 Medium-Fat Meat
	1/2 Fat

Ω   Ω   Ω   Ω

GROUND BEEF STROGANOFF

2 lbs. lean ground beef
2 med. onions, chopped
2 garlic cloves, minced
8 oz. fresh mushrooms, sliced
2 tsp. sodium-reduced, beef-flavored
   bouillon granules
1 cup water
1-1/2 cups plain low-fat yogurt
4 Tbsp. flour
3 Tbsp. tomato paste
1/2 tsp. salt
1/4 tsp. pepper

Brown meat in skillet; drain fat. Add onions, garlic and mushrooms and saute' until onion is golden. Place in crockpot. Dissolve bouillon granules in water. Mix together yogurt and flour. Add bouillon, yogurt, tomato paste, salt and pepper to crock pot. Cover and cook on low for 6 hours.* Serve hot over noodles or rice.

Simmer in Dutch oven for about 1 hour or bake at 350° for 1 hour.

Yield:	8 portions
Calories:	310
Fat:	12 g
Cholesterol:	74 mg
Sodium:	250 mg
Dietary Exchanges:.....	1 Skim Milk
	3 Medium-Fat Meat

HAMBURGER CUPCAKES

    1 lb. lean ground beef or
       ground turkey
    1 can mushroom soup or
       low fat sauce mix
    1/4 cup chopped onion
    1 egg beaten or 2 egg whites
    1/2 cup low fat grated American cheese
    1/2 cup bread crumbs (whole wheat)
    1/2 tsp. garlic powder
    1/2 tsp. dry mustard
    1/2 tsp. Worcestershire sauce

Combine ingredients and mix thoroughly. Trim crusts off 16-18 slices of bread sprayed with non-stick cooking spray. Place slices with cooking spray side down in muffin tins and shape. Fill with meat mixture and bake at 350° for 40 minutes.

Yield: .... 16 servings
Calories: 93
Fat: .... 5.07 g
Cholesterol: .... 18.87 mg
Sodium: .... 160 mg
Dietary Exchanges:..... 1 Medium-Fat Meat

HAZEL'S HAMBURGER HOTDISH

1 cup washed rice
1 cup whole kernel corn
1 cup drained green beans
1 sm. can tomato sauce (low salt)
1/2 cup water
1/2 cup diced green peppers
1/4 cup finely chopped onion
1 lb. browned extra lean ground beef
1 46 oz. can tomato juice (low salt)

Pre-heat oven to 350°. Place ingredients in large casserole with cover. Brown ground beef, drain fat. Mix uncooked rice, corn, green beans, tomato sauce, water, green peppers and onion. Add 1/2 of 46 oz. can of tomato juice. Bake on hour with cover. Uncover. Add remaining half of tomato juice. Finish baking for another 1/2 hour.

Yield: .... 16 servings
Calories: 156
Fat: .... 5.80 g
Cholesterol: .... 22.4 mg
Sodium: .... 33 mg
Dietary Exchanges:..... 1 Bread
                                        1 Vegetable

Hazel Bergsgaard

MEAT LOAVES ITALIANO

1 lb. lean ground beef
1 tsp. basil
1/4 tsp. garlic powder
1/4 tsp. fennel
1/2 tsp. oregano
1/4 tsp. brown sugar
8 oz. no added salt tomato sauce
2 oz. mozzarella cheese, grated
Fresh parsley garnish

Combine meat with basil, garlic, fennel, oregano, and brown sugar in a bowl. Mix well, then shape into 4 loaves. Put on microwave meat tray and MICROWAVE for 4 minutes on high or broil in oven or on grill for 20 to 25 minutes. Drain well, then transfer to oven-safe meat platter. Pour tomato sauce over loaves, top with shredded cheese, and broil for 4 to 6 minutes. Garnish with parsley before serving. Recipe can be doubled, prepared, and frozen.

Yield: .... 4 (4 oz.) servings
Calories: 203
Fat: .... 6 g
Cholesterol: .... 76 mg
Sodium: .... 121 mg
Dietary Exchanges:..... 3 Lean Meat
Preparation Time: .... 20 min.

MEXICAN BAKE

1/2 lb. extra lean hamburger
1-1/2 cups cooked red beans
1 sm. onion, chopped
1/2 tsp. salt
2 cloves garlic, minced
1/2 tsp. cumin
1 dried red pepper crumbled (optional)
1/2 tsp. chili powder
2 8-oz. cans tomato sauce
1 cup lowfat plain yogurt
1 cup lowfat cottage cheese
1 (3-4 oz.) can chopped green chilies
6 flour tortillas
2 cups part skim milk mozzarella, shredded

Cook hamburger and onion until crumbly. Drain well. Add beans, salt, garlic, cumin, red pepper, chili powder and tomato sauce. In a bowl, mix yogurt, cottage cheese and chilies. Bake tortillas on a cookie sheet at 400° until crisp and golden (approx. 5 minutes on each side.) Crush baked tortillas slightly. Put half the tortilla pieces in 2-1/2 quart casserole. Add half the meat mixture, half the yogurt mixture and sprinkle with half the cheese. Repeat, ending with the cheese. Bake, covered, at 350° for 30 to 35 minutes.

Yield: .... 8 (1 cup) servings
Calories: 282
Fat: .... 9 g
Sodium: .... 446 mg
Dietary Exchanges:..... 1-1/2 Breads
                         3 Lean Meats

MEXICAN CORN MAIN DISH

    1 lb. lean ground beef, browned
    4 ears fresh corn or
       1 10-oz. pkg. frozen corn, thawed
    1 egg or 1/4 cup liquid egg substitute
    1/2 cup nonfat yogurt
    1 cup shredded mozzarella cheese
    1/2 cup cornmeal
    1 7-oz. can diced green chilies
    1/4 tsp. garlic powder
    1/4 tsp. salt
    Chopped fresh parsley,
       as an optional garnish

Preheat oven to 350°F. Brown ground beef; drain well. Spray a 3-qt. casserole dish with nonstick cooking spray. Cut corn off the cob if necessary. Put yogurt and egg in blender. Puree well. Combine this with corn, browned meat, and all other ingredients in casserole dish. Sprinkle fresh parsley over the top as a garnish. Bake for 50 minutes or MICROWAVE on high for 20 minutes. This casserole is done when the center is firm and the top is lightly browned. This may be assembled, frozen or thawed for later baking.

Yield:	8 (3/4 cup) servings
Calories:	187
Fat:	5 g
Cholesterol:	40 mg
Sodium:	172 mg with salt
	109 mg without salt
Dietary Exchanges:.....	1 Bread/Starch
	2 Lean Meat
Preparation Time:	35 min. if microwaved

MOCK BREAKFAST SAUSAGE

1-1/2 lbs. lean ground beef
1/4 cup minced parsley
1 tsp. rubbed sage
1 tsp. paprika
1/2 tsp. onion powder
1/2 tsp. thyme leaves
1/2 tsp. fennel leaves
1/2 tsp. pepper

About 30 minutes before serving, in medium bowl, combine all ingredients; cover and refrigerate. (For extra flavor refrigerate over night). Shape into 18 small patties. Pan broil or oven broil until cooked through.

Yield: .... 18 portions
Calories: 78
Fat: .... 5.38 g
Cholesterol: .... 21.50 mg
Sodium: .... 17 mg
Dietary Exchanges:..... 1 Meat

NORTH DAKOTA CHILI

1 lb. lean ground beef
3 garlic cloves, minced
2 cups chopped onion
2 cups chopped celery with leaves
2 28-oz. cans whole tomatoes
3 Tbsp. chili powder
1/4 cup chopped parsley
1/2 tsp. pepper
2 16-oz. cans dark red kidney beans

In heavy saucepan or Dutch oven, brown meat. Add garlic, onion, and celery and cook until onion is golden. Break tomatoes into pieces and add along with juice to meat mixture. Add chili powder, parsley and pepper. Bring to a boil, reduce heat, cover and simmer for 2 hours. Shortly before serving, add kidney beans with liquid and heat thoroughly.

Yield:	12 cups
Calories:	173
Fat:	4.1 g
Cholesterol:	25 mg
Sodium:	767 mg
Dietary Exchanges:	1 Starch
	2 Vegetable
	1 Lean Meat

NUTRITION ALERT: This recipe is high in sodium. Reduce the sodium by draining and rinsing kidney beans before adding to chili mixture. Add water if necessary.

PIZZA MEAT LOAF

Serve with a salad and French bread.

> 1 lb. extra lean ground beef (9% fat or less)
>   or ground turkey (7% fat)
> 1/4 cup Pizza Sauce
> 1 oz. grated, part skim mozzarella cheese
> 1/2 cup thin sliced vegetables
>   (green pepper and onion)

Conventional Oven: Preheat oven to 425°. Spray a 9-inch pie plate with a non-stick cooking spray. Pat the meat into a pie plate. Bake for 12-14 minutes. Drain any liquid. Top with pizza sauce, cheese, and vegetables. Return to oven for 5 minutes.

Microwave Method: Spray a 9-inch glass pie plate with non-stick coating. Pat the meat into the pie plate. Cover with wax paper and cook on high for 6 minutes turning 1/4 turn halfway through cooking time. Drain any liquid. Top with pizza sauce, cheese, and vegetables. Cook on high for 2 minutes until cheese is melted.

Yield: .... 4 servings
Calories: .... 220 turkey
                               250 beef
Fat: .... 15 g
Cholesterol: .... 75 mg
Sodium: .... 160 mg
Dietary Exchanges:..... 1/2 Vegetable
                               3 Medium Fat Meat

TACO CASSEROLE

1 15-oz. can kidney beans,
   processed smooth in blender
1 lb. lean ground beef,
   browned and drained
1/2 tsp. garlic powder
1/2 tsp. cumin
1/4 tsp. cayenne (optional)
8 oz. no added salt tomato sauce
1/4 cup chopped onion
1/4 cup chopped green pepper
4 med. flour tortillas, cut into triangles
2 oz. part-skim American cheese, grated
Chili powder garnish

Preheat oven to 375° F. Spray a 9 x 13-inch dish or two 8 x8-inch baking dishes with nonstick cooking spray. Spread processed beans onto bottom of prepared pan. Combine browned meat with garlic, cumin, cayenne, and tomato sauce. Spread over beans. Top with onion, green pepper, tortilla triangles, and cheese. Sprinkle chili powder on top. Bake for 30 minutes or MICROWAVE for 20 to 22 minutes on medium-high power. Remove from oven and let stand for 5 minutes. Serve with chopped lettuce and tomato. This may be assembled and frozen for later baking.

Yield: .... 8 (1 cup) servings
Calories: 246
Fat: .... 7 g
Cholesterol: .... 19 mg
Sodium:.......................... 192 mg
Dietary Exchanges:....... 1 Bread/Starch
                                         2 Vegetable
                                         2 Lean Meat
Preparation Time: .... 40 minutes

ZUCCHINI LASAGNA CASSEROLE

1 lb. lean ground beef, browned and drained
4 sm. zucchini, peeled and sliced thin lengthwise
1 onion, chopped
1 green pepper, chopped
4 oz. mushrooms, sliced
1/2 tsp. vegetable oil
8 oz. no added salt tomato sauce
1/4 tsp. each garlic powder, fennel, and pepper
1 tsp. each basil and oregano
2 oz. mozzarella cheese, shredded
2/3 cup low-fat cottage cheese
1/3 cup Parmesan cheese

Preheat oven to 375° F. (Recipe can be microwaved.) Saute onion, pepper and mushrooms in oil in dutchoven or MICROWAVE 4 minutes in 2-quart casserole dish. Meanwhile, steam sliced zucchini 6 minutes on stove top or MICROWAVE with 1 Tbsp. water for 3 minutes in covered container. Stir meat, tomato sauce, and seasonings into sauteed vegetables. Combine cottage and mozzarella cheeses in separate bowl. Spray an 8-inch square baking dish with nonstick cooking spray. Layer zucchini, cheeses, and meat sauce twice. Sprinkle Parmesan cheese over last meat layer. Bake for 45 minutes or MICROWAVE 20 minutes. This can be assembled and frozen for later use.

Yield:	4 (1-1/2 cup) servings
Calories:	298
Fat:	9 g
Cholesterol:	77 mg
Sodium:	421 mg
Dietary Exchanges:	2 Vegetable
	3 Lean Meat
	1 Skim Milk
Preparation Time:	55 min. using microwave method

COMPANY STRATA

12 slices whole wheat bread,
   cut into 12 "donut and holes"
12 oz. pkg. sharp processed cheese
   sliced (low fat)
10 oz. pkg. frozen chopped broccoli,
   cooked and drained
2 cups fully cooked ham, diced
   extra lean (approx. 5% fat)
1-1/2 cups Egg Beaters
3-1/2 cups milk
2 Tbsp minced onion
1/2 tsp. salt
1/4 tsp. dry mustard

Fit the scraps of bread (top with crusts removed) in bottom of baking dish. Layer cheese, broccoli, and ham over bread. Arrange "donut and holes" atop. Combine remaining ingredients. Pour over bread, cover; refrigerate 6 hours. Bake in 9x13x2 inch pan for 55 minutes at 325° uncovered. Let stand 10 minutes before cutting.

Yield: .... 12 servings
Calories: 202
Fat: .... 4.64 g
Cholesterol: .... 27.42 mg
Sodium: .... 1037 mg
Dietary Exchanges: .... 1 Bread
                            1 Vegetable
                            2 Lean Meat

NUTRITION ALERT: This recipe is high in sodium. It is intended for occasional use only. Substitute turkey for ham, and omit 1/2 tsp. salt to reduce sodium.

❄   ❄   ❄   ❄   ❄

FAJITAS BARBEQUE STYLE

1 lb. top sirloin steak, 1 inch thick
Marinade:
1/3 cup lime juice
1/4 tsp. salt (optional)
1/2 tsp. garlic powder
1/4 tsp. pepper
1 tsp. dried oregano
1 tsp. chili powder
8 flour tortillas, 6-inch size
1 cup each: shredded lettuce
   and chopped tomato
1/2 cup sliced green onion
1 oz. grated, low fat cheddar cheese

Trim steak and place in a shallow bowl. Mix marinade ingredients and spread on both sides of steak. Refrigerate for 6-8 hours, turning halfway through marinating time. Drain marinade and discard. Broil or barbeque steak about 2-3 minutes on each side or until desired doneness. Carve crossgrain into thin slices. Heat tortillas in microwave or in a non-stick skillet. To serve, divide the meat, lettuce, tomato, onions, and cheese over 8 tortillas.

Yield:	8 filled tortillas
	4 (2 filled tortilla) servings
Calories:	360
Fat:	11 g
Cholesterol:	80 mg
Sodium:	198 mg
Dietary Exchanges:.....	2 Starch
	3-1/2 Lean Meat

HAM AND
VEGETABLE TORTILLA

Stuff 8 6-in. flour tortillas with a mixture of:

> 8 oz. slivered lean ham
> 2 oz. shredded part-skim cheese of choice
> 2 cups steamed vegetables of choice

Using flour tortillas

Flour tortillas are made for stuffing. For quickest results, stuff them, rolling seam side down and place in a pan that has been sprayed with nonstick cooking spray. Put them in the microwave for 2-1/2 to 4 minutes. Conventional baking at 375° F. for 20 minutes also works. Always serve chopped lettuce and/or tomatoes on the side. For a topping, try blenderized part-skim ricotta or nonfat cottage cheese.

Yield: .... 4 servings
Calories: 323
Fat: .... 15 g
Cholesterol: .... 35 mg
Sodium: .... 430 mg
Dietary Exchanges:..... 2 Starch/Bread
2 Lean Meat
1 Fat

* Superfast Recipe

HAM STEAK MARINADE

1/4 cup of each:
   Worcestershire sauce
   Brown sugar
   Lemon juice
1 lb. lean ham steak

Mix 1/4 cup each of Worcestershire sauce, brown sugar, and lemon juice. Marinate 1 lb. lean ham steak for 20 minutes, then broil.

Yield: .... 4 servings
Calories: 191
Fat: .... 4 g
Cholesterol: .... 74 mg
Sodium: .... 1388 mg
Dietary Exchanges:..... 1/2 Starch/Bread
                         3 Lean Meat

NUTRITION ALERT: This recipe is high in sodium. It is intended to be used for occasional use only.

* Superfast Recipe

MARINATED STEAK

1-1/2 lbs. boneless steak
   (round, flank, or top sirloin), well trimmed
Marinade:
1/3 cup soy sauce
1/3 cup chili sauce
1/4 cup water
1 Tbsp. Worcestershire sauce
1/4 tsp. pepper
1/4 tsp. garlic powder
1/8 tsp. chili powder
1 Tbsp. dried parsley
1 tsp. dried oregano
1/8 tsp. dry mustard

Mix marinade ingredients in a container large enough to accommodate the steak. Add steak, coating both sides with the mixture. Refrigerate and marinate for 2 to 4 hours, turning steak once halfway through the marinating time. Drain marinade. Barbeque or broil to desired doneness.

Yield: .... 6 servings
Calories: 190
Fat: .... 7 g
Cholesterol: .... 75 mg
Sodium: .... 609 mg
Dietary Exchanges:..... 3-1/2 Lean Meat

ORANGE PORK CHOPS

1/3 cup low sugar orange marmalade
2 Tbsp. Dijon mustard
4 pork rib chops (cut 3 per pound)
4 bunches of green onions

In a small saucepan mix marmalade and mustard. Stir over medium heat until marmalade is melted. Set aside. Trim all fat from chops. Place chops on rack of a broiler pan or use the outdoor barbeque. Broil about 4 inches from the heat for 6 minutes. Turn chops and broil for 2 more minutes. Spoon half of the glaze over chops. Broil 4 to 5 minutes more or until chops are no longer pink. Meanwhile, slice onions diagonally into 1-inch pieces. Spray a skillet with non-stick coating and stir-fry onions 2 minutes or until crisp-tender. Stir in remaining glaze and heat thoroughly. Serve over chops.

Yield: .... 4 servings
Calories: 220
Fat: .... 8 g
Cholesterol: .... 71 mg
Sodium: .... 293 mg
Dietary Exchanges:..... 2/3 Fruit
                          3 Lean Meat

ROUND STEAK IN BEER

1/2 tsp. garlic powder
1 tsp. sugar
1 can beer
1 lb. lean trimmed round steak

Mix garlic powder, sugar, and can of beer. Marinate lean trimmed round steak 20 minutes, then broil.

Yield: .... 4 servings
Calories: 192
Fat: .... 4 g
Cholesterol: .... 72 mg
Sodium: .... 56 mg
Dietary Exchanges:..... 1/2 Starch/Bread
3 Lean Meat

* Superfast Recipe

TERIYAKI-GLAZED PORK MEDALLIONS

1 tsp. margarine or butter
1 lb. (2 small) pork tenderloins, cut
    crosswise into 1/2-inch slices
2 Tbsp. brown sugar
2 Tbsp. orange juice
1 tsp. lite soy sauce
1/4 tsp. garlic powder
1/4 tsp. ginger

Melt margarine in large nonstick skillet over medium-high heat. Add pork; cook and stir until lightly browned and no longer pink, about 6 to 8 minutes. Drain if necessary. In small bowl; combine brown sugar, orange juice, soy sauce, garlic powder and ginger; blend well. Pour over pork; cook and stir until mixture thickens and coats pork.

Yield: .... 4 servings
Calories: 180
Fat: .... 5 g
Cholesterol: .... 66 mg
Sodium: .... 115 mg
Dietary Exchanges:..... 3 Lean Meat

WESTERN BROIL

1 lb. round steak,
   cut 1-inch thick
1/2 cup light soy sauce
2 Tbsp. honey
1 Tbsp. lemon juice
2 scallions, finely chopped
1/4 tsp. garlic powder
3/4 cup sliced carrots, steamed
1-1/2 cups pea pods, steamed

Combine soy sauce, honey, lemon juice, scallions and garlic powder in a small bowl. Place steak in a pie pan and pour marinade over the steak, turning to coat. Marinate in the refrigerator for at least 30 minutes or up to 24 hours. Discard the marinade. Place steak on a broiler rack, so surface of meat is 3 inches from the heat. Broil for 20 minutes, turning once. Meanwhile, arrange steamed carrots and peas around outside edges of a serving platter. Carve beef into 4 servings and place in the middle of platter. Serve.

Yield: .... 4 (8 oz.) servings
Calories: 240
Fat: .... 6 g
Cholesterol: .... 72 mg
Sodium: .... 692 mg
   (To reduce sodium, use 1/4 cup light soy sauce.)
Dietary Exchanges:..... 1 Vegetable
                        4 Lean Meat
Preparation Time: .... 60 min.

WILD RICE CASSEROLE

1/4 lb. Canadian bacon, cut up
1/2 stick sunflower margarine
1 lg. onion, diced
1 whole bunch celery, diced
1 jar whole button mushrooms
1 can mushroom stems and pieces
1 can chicken rice soup
   (reduced salt and reduced fat)
1-1/2 cup wild rice, cooked

Saute bacon, add vegetables and butter, cook until tender. Mix with cooked rice and soup. Bake 45 minutes.

Yield: .... 6 servings
Calories: 299
Fat: .... 10.82 g
Cholesterol: .... 10.21 mg
Sodium: .... 364 mg
Dietary Exchanges:..... 2 Breads
                                 1 Vegetable
                                 1 Medium-Fat Meat
                                 1 Fat

Bison/ Buffalo & Wild Game

Bison/Buffalo Meat:
Hearty and Healthy . . . To Eat!

Bison meat is considered a health food because it's higher in protein and lower in fat, cholesterol and calories than most meats, including poultry and some kinds of fish. In fact, buffalo meat contains less than 50 calories per ounce. Beef contains nearly four times the amount of fat buffalo does.

Although bison meat is similar to beef, it needs to be handled and cooked differently.

Some basic cooking tips to remember are: bison meat is not tough; with the low fat content, bison does not need to be cooked as long with as high a temperature as beef; remember "low and slow"; cook to the same doneness that you prefer in beef.

A few pointers to follow in preparing bison meat: broiling – move broiler rack down a notch from where you'd place it for beef. Check and turn your steaks a few minutes earlier than you normally would; roasting – if you normally roast beef at 325°, turn the temperature down to 275° for bison. Plan the same amount of cooking time as for a beef roast of comparable size. It may be finished cooking a little sooner.

3 oz.	Calories	Fat	Cholesterol
Bison*	93	1.8 g	43 mg
Turkey	125	3.0 g	59 mg
Beef	183	8.7 g	55 mg
Chicken	140	3.0 g	73 mg
American Heart Assoc. Recommendations:	177	7.7 g	77 mg

*Bison fed corn ration for 90 days prior to processing (unpublished data) information provided by the National Buffalo Association.

TASTY BISON BAKE

16 oz. pkg. Pasta Growers noodles
2 lbs. ground bison
2 (8 oz.) cans tomato sauce*
12 oz. ctn. small curd lowfat cottage cheese
1 (8 oz.) pkg. cream cheese (Use lowfat or fat free)
1/2 cup chopped onion
1 cup non-fat yogurt
3 Tbsp. minced green pepper

Preheat oven to 350° F. Coat rectangular baking dish or 9x13 pan with non-stick cooking spray. Cook noodles according to package and drain well. Brown bison in 1 Tbsp. of margarine, stir in tomato sauce, pepper to taste. Turn stove off and set aside.

Combine cottage cheese, cream cheese, yogurt, onions, and green peppers in mixing bowl. Spread half of the noodles in casserole dish and cover with cheese mixture. Then put on the rest of the noodles and cover with browned meat mixture. Bake for 30 minutes. Serve hot.

Yield: .... 8 servings
Calories: 596
Fat: .... 32.2 g
Cholesterol: .... 58 mg
Sodium: .... 984 mg
Dietary Exchanges: .... 2 Bread/Starch
4 Medium-Fat Meats
1 Milk
4 Fats

*Use salt-free or low salt tomato sauce to reduce sodium.

Nutrition Note: Nutritional analysis information is an approximate. This recipe is high in fat, as the serving sizes are very large. Decrease fat by reducing serving size and use fat-free cream cheese.

North American Bison Coop
New Rockford, ND

BUFFALO LASAGNA

1 lb. buffalo burger
1 clove garlic, minced
1 (6 oz.) can reduced-salt or salt-free tomato paste
1 Tbsp. basil

To prepare meat filling, brown burger with garlic, basil and salt. Add tomato paste and simmer uncovered for 30 minutes.

Cheese Filling:
3 cups non-fat cottage cheese
1/2 cup grated Parmesan cheese
2 Tbsp. parsley flakes
2 beaten egg whites
1/2 tsp. pepper
Dash salt

Slice thinly 1 lb. mozzarella cheese. Prepare lasagna noodles as directed on the package. Place half of the prepared noodles in the bottom of a 13x9 inch pan. Over the noodles, spread half of the cheese filling, half of the meat filling and half of the mozzarella. Lay rest of the noodles over the mozzarella. Repeat the procedure with the cheese, meat and mozzarella. Bake at 375° for 30 minutes. Let it stand for 40 minutes before cutting.

Yield: .... 6 servings
Calories: 346
Fat: .... 18 g
Cholesterol: .... 76 mg
Sodium: .... 678 mg
Dietary Exchanges: .... 2 Vegetable
                                          4 Lean Meat
                                          1 Fat

Nutrition Note: Nutritional analysis information is an approximate.

BISON LOAF

2 lb. ground bison
1-1/2 pkgs. soda crackers, finely chopped
2 egg whites
1/2 cup milk
1/2 med. onion, chopped
1/2 med. green pepper, chopped
3 Tbsp. salsa
Salt, pepper and garlic powder to taste

Mix all of the above ingredients and form into loaf.
Bake in 300° F oven approximately 45 minutes or
until done.

Yield: .... 8 servings
Calories: 376
Fat: .... 22 g
Cholesterol: .... 103 mg
Sodium: .... 288 mg
Dietary Exchanges:.... 1 Bread/Starch
                        4 Lean Meat
                        2 Fat

Nutritional Note: Nutritional analysis is an approximate.

The American Bison Association

BUFFALO ROAST

3 or 4 lb. buffalo roast
1 slice Canadian bacon, cut into small pieces
2 cloves garlic, crushed
Salt and pepper
1 bay leaf
2 cloves
1 cup orange juice

Cut slits in meat and insert small pieces of bacon and garlic. Salt and pepper well. Sear meat on all sides. Put meat in roaster and place bay leaf and cloves on top. Baste with orange juice. Roast in 325° oven until internal temperature reaches 170 degrees, basting frequently with orange juice.

Yield: .... 8 servings
Calories: 398
Fat: .... 16 g
Cholesterol: .... 164 mg
Sodium: .... 138 mg
Dietary Exchanges:.... 4 Lean Meat

Nutrition Note: Nutritional analysis information is an approximate.

BUFFALO SHISH KABOB

1-1/2 lbs. sirloin or top roast, cut in 1 to
   1-1/2 inch cubes
2 sm. (4 inch) yellow squash, thickly sliced
1 onion, thickly sliced (Optional)
1/3 cup olive oil
About 10 cherry tomatoes
1 green pepper, cut in 1 inch squares
12 lg. mushroom caps
14 tsp. freshly ground black pepper
1 or 2 cloves garlic, crushed (Optional)
1/3 cup white wine
Lemon wedges

Marinate meat and vegetables (except tomatoes) in mixture of seasonings, garlic, oil and wine for at least two hours at room temperature, overnight in refrigerator. Remove from marinade, arrange meat on skewers alternately with vegetables. Broil 5 inches from heat over charcoal or on rotisserie spit for approximately 7 to 10 minutes, or to desired doneness, turning frequently or continuously. (Vegetables soaked in oil mixture need no previous cooking.) Serve with lemon wedges, the lemon to be squeezed over the meat.

Yield: .... 8 servings
Calories: 287
Fat: .... 15 g
Cholesterol: .... 69 mg
Sodium:........................ 62.6 mg
Dietary Exchanges: .... 1/4 Vegetable
   3 Lean Meat

Nutrition Note: Nutritional analysis information is an approximate.

BUFFALO TACOS

1 lb. ground buffalo
1/2 clove garlic, minced
2 Tbsp. onion, grated
1/2 cup salsa
1 tsp. chili powder
12 tortillas or taco shells
Taco toppings of your choice
Taco sauce

Mix meat, garlic, grated onion, Worcestershire sauce, salt and chili powder, brown in skillet. Mixture should be moist; keep hot. Warm tortillas in microwave or oven. Allow each person to fill their own tortillas or taco shell with meat mixture and their choice of taco toppings.

TACO SAUCE: heat together 1 cup tomato juice, 3 Tbsp. catsup, 1/8 tsp. Tabasco sauce and 1/2 tsp. Worcestershire sauce.

Yield: .... 6 servings
Calories: 222
Fat: .... 15 g
Cholesterol: .... 66 mg
Sodium: .... 87 mg
Dietary Exchanges:.... 1 Bread/Starch
2 Lean Meat
1 Fat

Nutrition Note: Nutritional analysis information is an approximate.

TATANKA STROGANOFF

1/2 cup chopped onion
1/4 cup margarine
1 lb. ground bison
Garlic powder
2 Tbsp. flour
1/4 tsp. pepper
1/4 tsp. paprika (Optional)
4 oz. fresh mushrooms
1 can cream of chicken soup diluted with
   1 can skim milk (more if desired)
1 cup non-fat yogurt

Saute onion in margarine until golden. Stir in bison and brown; add garlic, flour, pepper, paprika, and mushrooms. Saute for about 5 minutes. Add soup and milk and simmer uncovered 10 minutes. When ready to serve, stir in sour cream. Serve over noodles or rice.

Yield: .... 5 servings
Calories: 282
Fat: .... 17 g
Cholesterol: .... 69 mg
Sodium:......................... 507 mg
Dietary Exchanges:........ 3 Lean Meat
                              1 Milk
                              1 Fat

Nutrition Note: Nutrition analysis is approximate on all bison recipes. Substitute a low-sodium cream soup to reduce sodium.

North American Bison Coop
New Rockford, ND

DON'S PHEASANT CASSEROLE

1 sm. box instant brown and wild rice
2 cups chopped cooked pheasant
1/3 cup chopped water chestnuts
1/3 cup cream soup substitute or lowfat,
   low salt canned cream soup
1 sm. can mushrooms, well drained
1-3/4 cups water

Steam or boil pheasant until tender. Cool and remove from the bone, chopping into bite-sized pieces. Cook the rice according to package directions. While the rice is cooking, preheat oven to 350° F. Spray a 2-qt. casserole dish with nonstick cooking spray. Mix 1/3 cup cream soup substitute with 1-3/4 cups water. Transfer cooked rice, meat, water chestnuts, drained mushrooms, and soup and water mixture to the dish and stir. Bake uncovered for 30 minutes.

Yield:	4 (4 oz.) servings
Calories:	294
Fat:	4 g
Cholesterol:	39 mg
Sodium:	397 mg
Dietary Exchanges:	1-1/2 Bread/Starch
	1 Vegetable
	3 Lean Meat
Preparation Time:	45 minutes, if pheasant is precooked

GARY'S ROAST VENISON IN THE CROCKPOT

2 lb. venison
2 Tbsp. flour
1 Tbsp. oil
1/2 tsp. garlic powder
1 lg. onion, sliced
2 Tbsp. brown sugar
1 tsp. mustard
1 Tbsp. Worcestershire sauce
1/4 cup lemon juice
1 (16 oz.) can no salt added tomatoes

Marinade:
1/2 cup vinegar
1/2 tsp. garlic powder
2 Tbsp. salt
Cold water to cover meat

Mix vinegar, garlic powder, and salt together. Place meat in a deep flat pan. Pour cold water over meat and add vinegar mixture. Marinate overnight. Remove from marinade and drain well. Roll meat in flour and brown in 1 Tbsp. vegetable oil in a skillet. Transfer browned meat to the crockpot. Add all remaining ingredients and cook on low for 8 hours. This makes an excellent leftover.

Yield:	8 (4 oz.) servings
Calories:	291
Fat:	10 g
Cholesterol:	65 mg
Sodium:	86 mg
Dietary Exchanges:	1-1/2 Bread/Starch
	3 Lean Meat
Preparation Time:	Overnight marinade
	8 hours in crockpot

Speed Alert: For best results with venison, marinate overnight.

VENISON INDIAN SUMMER ROAST

1 (3 lb.) shoulder roast
Pepper
1/2 tsp. nutmeg
1/4 cup flour
1 med.-sized oven cooking bag
1 cup apple cider

Sprinkle the venison roast with a bit of salt and pepper and then rub it into the meat with your fingers. Now sprinkle the nutmeg on top of the roast. Shake the four inside the oven bag, carefully set the roast inside, then pour the apple cider into the bottom of the bag. Close the bag with a twist-tie and make six inch-long slits on the top, then roast in a 325° oven for 2 hours. Transfer the roast to a hot plate, slice, then pour the cider gravy over the top. This may also be cooked in the crock pot for 6 to 8 hours on low or 4 to 6 hours on high.

Yield:	6 servings
Calories:	370
Fat:	5.16 g
Cholesterol:	147 mg
Sodium:	160 mg
Dietary Exchanges:	4 Lean Meat

MONTANA HIGH-COUNTRY BUTTERMILK VENISON

2 lbs. tenderloin or sirloin tip steaks
1 tsp. olive oil
1 cup buttermilk
1 Tbsp. flour

Cut the steak into thick cubes, then pound each with a meat hammer so it is no more than 1/2 inch thick. Place the meat in a bowl and cover with the buttermilk. Allow the steak to soak for 2 hours, then dredge the pieces in flour and panfry in 1 tsp. olive oil.

Yield: .... 8 servings
Calories: 186
Fat: .... 3.34 g
Cholesterol: .... 74.8 mg
Sodium: .... 112 mg
Dietary Exchanges:.... 4 Meat

VENISON TERIYAKI WITH RICE

2 lbs. tenderloin steak sliced into thin strips
2 Tbsp. olive oil
2 Tbsp. soy sauce
1/2 tsp. garlic powder
1 Tbsp. lemon juice
1 Tbsp. brown sugar
2 cups uncooked Minute Rice
4 oz. fresh mushrooms
1 cup green peppers, sliced into strips
1 cup beef broth or beef bouillon
   (reduced sodium)

Add the olive oil and soy sauce to a wok or high-sided skillet, then stir in the garlic, lemon juice, and brown sugar. Heat the wok or skillet on medium-high heat until the liquid begins to steam. Add the tenderloin strips and stir-fry them until they are almost cooked. Meanwhile, prepare the Minute Rice according to the instructions on the package. Now add to the wok or skillet the mushrooms (drained), green peppers, and beef broth. Turn the heat down to medium, cover, and slowly cook until everything is steaming hot. Then ladle over a bed of rice on a preheated platter. This recipe can also be cooked in the crock pot without the Minute Rice.

Yield:	6 servings	8 servings
Calories:	401	300
Fat:	8.06 g	6.04 g
Cholesterol:	98.3 mg	73.7 mg
Sodium:.....................	454 mg	341 mg
Dietary Exchanges:....	1 Bread	
	3 Lean Meat	
	1 Fat	

Breads

&

Muffins

HERBED CORN BREAD

  1 (8-1/2 oz.) box corn bread mix
  1/4 cup nonfat cottage cheese
  2 Tbsp. dried parsley
  2 Tbsp. dried chopped chives
  1 tsp. sage

Preheat oven to 350° F. Prepare mix according to package directions. Stir in cottage cheese, parsley, chives and sage. Pour batter into an 8-inch square pan. Bake for 25 minutes or until lightly browned. Cool and cut into 8 squares. Serve with syrup.

Yield: .... 8 servings
Calories: 118
Fat: .... 3 g
Cholesterol: .... 1 mg
Sodium: .... 300 mg
Dietary Exchanges:.... 1 Bread/Starch
                        1 Fat
Preparation Time: ...... 35 minutes

DATE NUT BREAD

8 oz. dates, chopped
1/2 cup chopped walnuts
1 cup raisins
1 tsp. baking soda
1 cup boiling water
2 cups flour
3/4 cup sugar
1 tsp. baking powder
1 egg or 1/4 cup liquid egg substitute

Preheat oven to 350° F. Spray 1 loaf pan with non-stick cooking spray. Combine dates, nuts, and raisins in a bowl. Sprinkle baking soda over this and then pour boiling water over the mixture and cover. Set aside. In a mixing bowl, use a pastry cutter to combine flour, sugar, baking powder, and egg or substitute. Add date and liquid mixture and blend well. Pour in prepared loaf pan. Bake for 50 to 60 minutes.

Yield: .... 16 servings
Calories: 168
Fat: .... 3 g
Cholesterol: .... 16 mg with egg
Sodium: .... 71 mg
                             1 Fruit
                             1 Bread/Starch
.... 1/2 Fat
Preparation Time: ...... 60 minutes

ONION CHEESE SUPPER BREAD

1/2 cup onion, chopped
1 egg, beaten
1/2 cup skim milk
1-1/2 cups biscuit mix
1 cup part-skim American cheese, shredded
2 Tbsp. parsley, chopped

Preheat oven to 400° F. In a small mixing bowl, combine egg and milk using an egg beater. In a large mixing bowl, combine chopped onion, biscuit mix, parsley, and 1/2 of the shredded cheese. Pour liquid into the large bowl and stir just until moist. Spread dough into an 8-inch round pan that has been sprayed with nonstick cooking spray. Spread remaining cheese over the top. Bake for 20 minutes.

Yield: .... 8 servings
Calories: 135
Fat: .... 6 g
Cholesterol: .... 42 mg with egg
20 mg with substitute
Sodium: .... 222 mg
Dietary Exchanges:.... 1 Bread/Starch
1 Fat
Preparation Time: ...... 35 minutes

❋ ❋ ❋

SUPER QUICK
STICKY ROLLS

1/4 cup 40% extra-light margarine, melted
1/4 cup firmly packed brown sugar
1 Tbsp. corn syrup
1 (11 oz.) can refrigerated soft breadsticks
1 Tbsp. sugar
1/2 tsp. cinnamon

Heat oven to 375°. In small bowl, combine margarine, brown sugar and corn syrup; blend well. Spread evenly in bottom of ungreased 8- or 9-inch round pan. Remove dough from can. Separate into 8 coils; DO NOT UNROLL BREADSTICKS. In shallow dish, combine sugar and cinnamon; dip one side of each coil into sugar-cinnamon mixture. Arrange coils, sugared side down, in pan. Sprinkle with any remaining sugar mixture. Bake for 19 to 24 minutes or until deep golden brown. Cool 1 minute; invert onto serving plate. Serve warm.

Yield:	8 servings
Calories:	170
Fat:	6 g
Cholesterol:	0 mg
Sodium:	310 mg
Dietary Exchanges:	1 Starch
	1/2 Fruit
	1 Fat

SOUTHWESTERN BREADSTICKS

2 Tbsp. cornmeal
1 tsp. chili powder
1 (11 oz.) pkg. refrigerated soft breadsticks
1 egg white, beaten

Heat oven to 350° F. In small bowl, combine cornmeal and chili powder. Unroll dough; separate into strips. Twist strips and place 1 inch apart on spray-coated cookie sheet. Brush with egg white; sprinkle with cornmeal mixture. Bake for 15 to 18 minutes or until golden brown.

Yield: .... 8 (1 breadstick) servings
Calories: 110
Fat: .... 3 g
Cholesterol: .... 0 mg
Sodium: .... 240 mg
Dietary Exchanges:.... 1 Starch
1/2 Fat

APPLE DRESSING

2 cups bread crumbs
4 cups chopped apples
1 sm. onion, chopped
3 stalks celery, chopped
1/4 cup raisins
1/2 cup apple juice
2 Tbsp. brown sugar
1/4 tsp. salt
1 tsp. cinnamon
2 Tbsp. margarine, melted

Preheat oven to 350° F. Combine crumbs, apple, onion, celery, and raisins in a 3-qt. baking pan that has been sprayed with nonstick cooking spray. In a small mixing bowl, combine remaining ingredients, stirring to blend. Pour liquid over bread mixture and toss to coat. Cover and bake for 35 minutes. Uncover and bake 10 more minutes to promote crusting.

Yield: .... 8 (1 cup) servings
Calories: 169
Fat: .... 1 g
Cholesterol: .... 0 mg
Sodium: .... 265 mg
Dietary Exchanges:.... 1 Fruit
                       1-1/2 Bread/Starch
Preparation Time: ...... 60 minutes

FRUIT STUFFING

1 cup chopped cranberries
2 Tbsp. sugar
12 slices raisin bread, cut into cubes
1 cup no added salt chicken or turkey broth
2 Tbsp. margarine, melted
2 tsp. grated orange peel
1/8 tsp. salt
2 Tbsp. orange juice

Preheat oven to 325° F. Combine all ingredients in a mixing bowl, stirring to moisten bread. Stuff turkey loosely and roast, or stir and transfer to a casserole dish that has been sprayed with nonstick cooking spray. Bake for 35 minutes, removing the cover the last ten minutes to brown.

Yield:	8 (3/4 cup) servings
Calories:	141
Fat:	4 g
Cholesterol:	0 mg
Sodium:	203 mg
Dietary Exchanges:	1 Bread/Starch
	1 Fat
Preparation Time:	60 minutes

FANCY APPLESAUCE BRAN MUFFINS

3 cups bran cereal
2 cups skim milk
1 cup unsweetened applesauce
2 eggs or 1/2 cup liquid egg substitute
1/3 cup vegetable oil
2-1/2 cups flour
4 tsp. baking powder
1/2 tsp. salt
3/4 cup brown sugar
1 Tbsp. cinnamon
1 tsp. grated lemon peel

Topping:
1/4 cup brown sugar
2 Tbsp. margarine

Preheat oven to 375° F. In large mixing bowl, combine cereal, milk, and applesauce and allow to sit 10 minutes. Beat in eggs and oil. In separate bowl, stir together all remaining dry ingredients. Fold dry ingredients into cereal mixture, just until moistened. Spoon into 24 muffin tins sprayed with nonstick cooking spray. Combine margarine and sugar for topping and sprinkle on top of muffins. Bake for 15 to 18 minutes.

Yield:	24 muffins
Calories:	154 per muffin
Fat:	5 g
Cholesterol:	23 mg
Sodium:	175 mg
Dietary Exchanges:	1 Bread/Starch
	1/2 Fruit
	1 Fat
Preparation Time:	40 minutes

APRICOT MUFFINS

2 cups flour
1/4 cup white sugar
1/2 cup brown sugar
1 Tbsp. baking powder
3/4 tsp. salt
2 tsp. pumpkin pie spice
1/2 cup oatmeal
1 cup chopped dried apricots
1/2 cup chopped walnuts
1 egg or 1/4 cup liquid egg substitute
1-1/2 cups skim milk
1/3 cup vegetable oil

Preheat oven to 350° F. Combine flour, brown sugar, baking powder, salt, pumpkin pie spice, and oatmeal in a large bowl. Stir in apricots and walnuts. Use an egg beater to combine eggs, milk, and oil in a small bowl. Pour liquid into dry ingredients, stirring just to moisten. Spoon batter into muffin cups, filling two-thirds full. Bake for 25 to 30 minutes or until muffins are brown.

Yield: .... 24 muffins
Calories: .... 199 per muffin
Fat: .... 5 g
Cholesterol: .... 14 mg with real eggs
Sodium: .... 120 mg
Dietary Exchanges:.... 1 Bread/Starch
                         1 Fat
Preparation Time: ...... 45 minutes

LEE'S "PRESCRIPTION" BRAN MUFFINS

Dry Ingredients:
2 cups oatmeal
1 cup miller's bran
1 cup flour
1/3 cup raisins
1 tsp. baking soda
1 tsp. cinnamon
3 Tbsp. granulated sugar substitute

Wet Ingredients:
1/8 cup oil (canola
  or sunflower)
1 egg or 1/4 cup
  egg substitute
1-3/4 cups skim milk

Mix dry ingredients together in a large bowl by hand. Mix wet ingredients together in another bowl, then mix into dry ingredients. Bake at 350° F for 25 minutes.

These muffins are (relatively) low-fat, low cholesterol, and full of fiber. Eat only one a day until you're used to them.

Yield:	12 muffins
Calories:	156 per muffin
Fat:	3.77 g
Cholesterol:	.64 mg
Sodium:	100 mg
Dietary Exchanges:....	2 Breads

PINEAPPLE BRAN MUFFINS

1 cup 100% wheat and bran cereal
1/2 cup shreds of whole bran cereal
1/2 cup boiling water
1 cup buttermilk*
1-1/2 tsp. baking soda
1/4 cup canola oil
1 egg
1-1/4 cups all purpose flour
3/4 cup firmly packed brown sugar
1/2 cup chopped fresh pineapple or
    well-drained canned crush pineapple
    in its own juice

Heat oven to 375° F. Spray 18 muffin cups with nonstick cooking spray or line with paper baking cups. Combine cereals in medium bowl; pour boiling water over cereals to soften. Set aside.

In large bowl, combine buttermilk, baking soda, oil and egg; beat until well blended. Lightly spoon flour into measuring cup; level off. Add flour and brown sugar; mix well. Stir in softened cereals and pineapple. Fill spray-coated muffin cups 3/4 full.

Bake for 18 to 22 minutes or until tops spring back when touched lightly in center.

*TIP: To substitute for buttermilk, use 1 Tbsp. vinegar or lemon juice plus milk to make 1 cup.

HIGH ALTITUDE: Above 3500 Feet: Increase flour to 1-1/3 cups. Bake as directed above.

Yield:	18 muffins
Calories:	120 per muffin
Fat:	4 g
Cholesterol:	12 mg
Sodium:	130 mg
Dietary Exchanges:	1 Starch
	1 Fat

REFRIGERATOR BRAN MUFFINS*

2 cups bran nugget cereal
2 cups boiling water
1 cup egg substitute (equal to 4 eggs)
4 cups buttermilk
2-1/2 cups sugar
1 cup oil (canola)
3 cups whole wheat flour
2 cups unbleached flour
5 tsp. baking soda
1-1/4 tsp. salt (optional)
2 cups dried fruit (optional)
4 cups Bran cereal

In a small bowl, pour boiling water over the bran nugget cereal and let stand until softened. In a large bowl, mix eggs, buttermilk, sugar and oil. Add the All Bran/water mixture to the egg mixture. Stir in the next four ingredients, just until moistened. If using dried fruit, add during this stage. Stir in Brand Buds or 100% Bran cereal. Batter may be covered and stored in refrigerator for up to three weeks and baked as needed.

Conventional Oven: Preheat oven to 375° F. Pour about 1/4 cup batter into muffin tins sprayed with non-stick coating or tins lined with cupcake papers. Bake for 15 minutes (20 minutes for chilled batter).

Microwave Method: For one muffin: Pour 1/4 cup batter in cupcake paper. Cook on high 55 to 70 seconds, rotating 1/4 turn halfway through cooking.

Yield:	56 muffins
Calories:	140 per muffin
Fat:	5 g
Cholesterol:	1 mg
Sodium:	181 mg
Dietary Exchanges:	1-1/2 Starch, 1/2 Fat

*People with diabetes should limit the use of this recipe because it contains significant amounts of sugar.

CORN MUFFINS

1-1/2 cups all purpose flour
1/2 cup cornmeal
2 Tbsp. sugar
3 tsp. baking powder
1/4 tsp. salt
1 (7 oz.) can golden whole kernel corn,
    well drained
1 cup milk
3 Tbsp. oil
1 egg, beaten

Heat oven to 400° F. Line 12 muffin cups with paper baking cups. Lightly spoon flour into measuring cup; level off. In medium bowl, combine flour, cornmeal, sugar, baking powder and salt; mix well. Stir in corn. In small bowl, combine milk, oil and egg; blend well. Add to dry ingredients; stir just until dry ingredients are moistened. Divide batter evenly among paper-lined muffin cups. Bake for 18 to 23 minutes or until golden brown. Cool 1 minute; remove from pan. Serve warm. HIGH ALTITUDE: Above 3500 Feet: No change.

Yield: .... 12 muffins
Calories: .... 140 per muffin
Fat: .... 5 g
Cholesterol: .... 19 mg
Sodium: .... 170 mg
Dietary Exchanges:.... 1 Starch
                             1/2 Fruit

MORNING GLORY MUFFINS

  6 cups all-purpose flour
  3-3/4 cups sugar
  2 Tbsp. baking soda
  3 Tbsp. cinnamon
  6 cups grated carrots
  1-1/2 cups raisins
  3 apples, grated
  18 egg whites, lightly beaten
   (or 2-1/4 cups egg substitute)
  3 cups applesauce
  2 Tbsp. vanilla

Combine dry ingredients. Stir in carrots, raisins and apples. Mix together egg whites, applesauce and vanilla. Combine all ingredients. Fill to top of muffin cups. Bake at 350° F. for 20 minutes.

Yield: .... 36 very large muffins
Calories: .... 207 per muffin
Fat: .... 0.25 g
Cholesterol: .... 0 mg
Sodium: .... 172 mg
Dietary Exchanges:.... 1 Bread
         1 Vegetable
         1 Fruit

OAT AND BLUEBERRY MUFFINS

2-1/2 cups oatmeal, uncooked,
   old-fashioned or quick
2 tsp. baking powder
1/2 tsp. cinnamon
1 cup fresh blueberries
2/3 cup skim milk
3 Tbsp. vegetable oil
2 egg whites, slightly beaten
1 Tbsp. brown sugar

Heat oven to 400° F. Place oats in blender or food processor bowl; cover and blend or process about 1 minute, stopping occasionally to stir. Line 12 muffin cups with baking cups. Combine ground oats, brown sugar, baking powder, salt and cinnamon. Add blueberries, milk, oil and egg whites; mix just until dry ingredients are moistened. Fill muffin cups almost full. Bake 20 to 25 minutes or until deep golden brown.

Yield: .... 12 muffins
Calories: .... 94 per muffin
Fat: .... 3 g
Cholesterol: .... .110 mg
Sodium: .... 59.5 mg
Dietary Exchanges:.... 1 Bread

Noreen Thomas
Dakota Medical Center

Cooking
For
One
or Two

GETTING READY TO COOK FOR ONE OR TWO
Simple Strategies for Making It Work

FRESH FOOD

Do you avoid buying fresh vegetables because you think they'll spoil in your refrigerator before you can use them? Before you cross fresh fruits and vegetables off your shopping list, try these suggestions.

- Shop with a friend. Try sharing the head of lettuce or bunch of celery.
- Wash vegetables when ready to use; they will last longer. A head of lettuce, however may be washed all at once. Store remaining lettuce in a plastic bag. It will keep about four days.
- Buy fruits and vegetables in season - they will be cheaper.
- Pop unused portions of red and green peppers into a freezer bag to use in casseroles and other cooked dishes.
- If you're too busy to peel and chop, buy small portions of fresh chopped vegetables from the grocery store salad bar. Some vitamins may be lost due to the advance slicing, but these are still a nutritious choice.
- Choose fresh vegetables that keep well for a week or more: artichokes, beets, cabbage, carrots, celery, parsnips, potatoes, winter squash, and sweet potatoes.
- Choose fresh fruit varieties that keep well or are easily used: apples, bananas, citrus fruits, grapes, melons, nectarines, peaches, and pears.
- Keep fruit that doesn't need to be refrigerated on the table where you will see it and remember to eat it.
- Fresh produce is great, but don't be afraid to shop for frozen vegetables.

SPICING UP CONVENIENCE FOODS

- Add fresh mushrooms, and peppers to bottled or canned onions to spaghetti sauce.
- Add a single-serving can of tuna to the pasta salad at the grocery store deli counter.
- Top frozen pizza with lots of tomatoes, peppers, or mushrooms.
- Add grated lowfat cheese to quick-cooking grits.
- Add fresh onions, pepper, tomatoes, and a small amount of cooked sliced chicken or turkey to bottled Mexican salsa.
- Add lemon juice and your favorite salsa to frozen corn.
- Add fresh fruit to plain lowfat yogurt.
- Add fresh onions, peppers, beans, and tomato sauce to quick-cooking rice.
- Add parmesan cheese to pasta or noodles and serve.
- Add garbanzos instead of Tuna or Hamburger to "Helper" meals. (Use only 1/2 of the box of these "Helper" meals. This will reduce salt, plus give you 2 meals from one box of "Helper mix".)
- Add diced onion, celery, carrots, a touch of garlic powder, and a hint of lemon juice to spice up canned tomato soup.
- Add broccoli florets, mushrooms, and a bit of grated cheese to a microwave "baked" potato.

EASY COOKING FOR ONE OR TWO

- Stir-fry pre-chopped vegetables from the grocery salad bar and serve with rice and beans.
- Steam pre-chopped vegetables and season with your favorite spices or low-sodium bouillon.
- Use your crockpot. Dump diced chicken, vegetables, and spices into a crockpot in the morning and come home at night to the warm, homey aroma of a hearty, ready-to-eat stew.
- For breakfast, try a sandwich of thinly spread peanut butter with banana on whole wheat bread, bagel, or pita.
- Use your imagination to create super-spuds. Top white or sweet potatoes with nonfat plain or lemon yogurt, nonfat or lowfat yogurt cheese, lowfat cheese (no more than 5 grams fat per ounce), barbecue sauce, lowfat butter substitutes, sauteed.
- Onions and vegetables, kidney beans, chili, or vegetable, lentil, or lowfat cream soups.
- Prepare extra when cooking rice, potato or pasta dishes. These can be refrigerated or frozen and used later.
- When making an oven meal, bake potatoes or muffins at the same time for later use.
- Use your microwave. It can help reduce kitchen mess and cooking time. Microwave meals can be prepared with less fat, too, by adding bouillon, wine, or broths. Your microwave is also your friend when it comes to thawing the meals you've frozen.
- Use pasta or a quick-cooking brown rice as the base for a terrific one-dish meal. While the pasta or rice cooks, quickly chop up a few of your favorite raw vegetables and chunks of cooked chicken or turkey (leftover, or from the deli). Mix everything together and cool just add your favorite lowfat dressing for a great chefs salad. You can substitute canned kidney or garbanzo beans a bit of lowfat cheese for the poultry, if you like. Or stir-fry or steam vegetables and poultry quickly, combine with warm pasta or rice, and top with tomato sauce, Mexican salsa, or a bit of lowfat Italian dressing.

CHEESE SOUFFLE-FILLED POTATOES

1 med. unpeeled baking potato (about 8 oz.)
2 Tbsp. skim milk
Dash of pepper
1/2 cup (2 oz.) shredded reduced-fat
  Cheddar cheese
1 Tbsp. canned chopped green chili
1 egg white

Bake potato at 400° for 1 hour or until done. Cool slightly. Cut baked potato in half lengthwise and carefully scoop pulp into a bowl, leaving shells intact. Add milk and pepper to potato pulp and beat at high speed with electric mixer until smooth. Stir in cheddar cheese and green chile; set aside. Beat egg white (at room temperature) at high speed until soft peaks form. Fold egg white into potato mixture. Fill shells with potato mixture and place on a baking sheet. Bake at 375° F for 27 minutes or until puffed.

Yield: .... 2 servings
Calories: 189
Fat: .... 5 g
Cholesterol: .... 21 mg
Sodium: .... 249 mg
Dietary Exchanges:..... 1 Bread/Starch
                                    1 Meat

FRUITED PORK AND PASTA SALAD

1/4 lb. lean boneless pork,
    about 1/4 inch thick
1-1/4 oz. (1/2 cup) uncooked Pasta Growers
    rotini (spiral pasta)
1/2 cup frozen cauliflower, sugar snap
    peas and carrots
    (from 16 oz. pkg.), thawed
1/2 cup cantaloupe cubes or balls
1 Tbsp. sliced green onions

Dressing:
1/3 cup lowfat orange yogurt
1 tsp. honey
1/4 tsp. salt
1/8 to 1/4 tsp. ginger
1/3 cup fresh strawberries

Spray small non-stick skillet with non-stick cooking spray; heat over medium-high heat until hot. Add pork; cook 4 to 7 minutes or until no longer pink, turning once. Cool slightly; slice or cube cooked pork. Set aside. Cook rotini to desired doneness as directed on package. Drain; rinse with cold water. In medium bowl, combine cooked rotini, pork, vegetables, cantaloupe and onions. In small bowl, combine all dressing ingredients except raspberries; blend well. Pour dressing over rotini mixture; toss gently to coat. To serve, spoon onto individual serving plates; garnish with raspberries.

Yield: .... 2 servings
Calories: 220
Fat: .... 3 g
Cholesterol: .... 35 mg
Sodium: .... 330 mg
Dietary Exchanges: .... 1 Starch
                                        1 Fruit
                                        1-1/2 Lean Meat

STRAWBERRY ORANGE CHICKEN SALAD

Dressing
1/4 cup strawberry syrup
1 Tbsp. red wine vinegar

Salad
2 cups torn spinach*
2 cups torn lettuce*
3/4 cup sliced cooked chicken,
    cut into strips**

2/3 cup sliced or halved fresh strawberries
    1 orange, peeled, seeded, cut up

In small bowl, combine dressing ingredients; mix well. In medium bowl, combine all salad ingredients; toss well. Spoon salad onto serving plates; drizzle with dressing.

TIPS: * If desired, packaged salad mix, found in the produce section of most large supermarkets, can be substituted for the spinach and lettuce.

** One chicken breast (2 chicken breast halves) will yield about 3/4 to 1 cup cubed cooked chicken. To cook 2 chicken breast halves, place chicken, skin side up, in 9-inch microwave-safe pie pan; place thickest portions toward outside edges of pie pan. Cover with microwave-safe waxed paper. Microwave on HIGH for 4 to 7 minutes or until chicken is fork tender and juices run clear, turning breast halves over once halfway through cooking. Smoked turkey or canned albacore tuna can be substituted for the cooked chicken.

Yield:	2 servings
Calories:	290
Fat:	5 g
Cholesterol:	47 mg
Sodium:	125 mg
Dietary Exchanges:	2 Fruit
	1 Vegetable
	2 Lean Meat

Crockpot Entrees, Soups & Stews

WHY COOK IN A CROCK?

We all know the reasons for using a crock:
It stretches time.
It assures controlled cooking, without our having
   to think about it.
It saves fuel.
It keeps the kitchen cool.
It makes inexpensive cuts of meats succulent
   and tasty.
It retains vitamins and minerals in the juices.
It's an enormous convenience in special situations,
   such as a vacation cabin or a boat galley.
It's a cinch to clean.

Cooking In The Crock Pot

Seasoning is the critical point when cooking with the
crock pot. Lightly add salt and pepper at the beginning,
not at the end. Use seasoning with care: lemon juice,
browned onions, dehydrated onions, garlic, lots of freshly
ground pepper, chopped parsley, and good herbs. Use
dried whole leaf herbs; fresh and ground herbs tend to
lose flavor in the crock.

Browning is an excellent idea. This cuts down on cooking time and adds much-needed color and adds flavor,
too.

Liquid, as a general rule in the crock pot should be one-
third less than in conventional recipes. Juice is pulled
from all the ingredients in the crock pot. Conventional
sauces will thin out in the crock and need the help of
creamed soups (the low fat, low salt), and the low fat
cottage cheese.

Cooking In The Crock Pot (Continued)

Quantities in the crock should never be less than one-quarter full. However, if covered with liquid, hard-to-cook things like vegetables don't cook successfully in the upper quarter of the crock pot. Sometimes it is a good idea to reverse the order, top to bottom halfway through the cooking time. This helps for more even cooking.

Keeping foods hot is not the prime function in a crockpot. Some foods will hold for one to two hours, but will begin to thin out after an hour or more.

Reheating foods in the crockpot to a temperature of 185° to 190° requires about 2-1/2 hours on low or one hour on high. If you are putting chilled food in the crockpot, add about 15 minutes to low or 8 to 10 minutes to high.

Before placing food in the crockpot, for easy cleanup, spray inside with a non-stick vegetable spray.

CROCK POT TIME GUIDE

If recipe says:	Cook in Crock Pot:
15 - 30 minutes	1-1/2 to 2 hours on high OR 4 - 8 hours on low
35 - 45 minutes	3 -4 hours on high OR 6 - 10 hours on low
50 min. - 3 hours	4 - 6 hours on high OR 8 to 18 hours on low

CARROT POT ROAST

This is a homey but very "honorable" pot roast, and one that most children think is great. (If you don't eat all the liquid at a meal, it makes a great soup.)

> 2-1/2 lbs. very lean round roast
> 2 onions, diced
> 3 cups fresh tomatoes
> 1 cup dry red wine, or water
> 3 bay leaves
> 1 tsp. celery powder
> 1/2 tsp. garlic powder
> Pepper
> 10 carrots, cut in "pennies"

Brown meat in skillet with non-stick finish. Remove to deep kettle. Drain off any fat, and cook onions, lightly, in skillet. Add onions to kettle, along with everything but the carrots. Bring to a boil, cover, and simmer 30 minutes. Add carrots, and simmer 1 to 1-1/2 hours more. Serves 8.

Yield:	8 servings
Calories:	318
Fat:	10.9 g
Cholesterol:	115 mg
Sodium:	108 mg
Dietary Exchanges:....	1 Vegetable
	4 Lean Meat

CROCKPOT CHEESE & POTATO CASSEROLE

2 lb. pkg. frozen fat-free hash browns,
    partly thawed
1 (No. 303) can cream style corn
    (Use no added salt for low salt diet)
1 cup lowfat yogurt (plain)
1/4 cup shredded fat-free Cheddar cheese
1 cup skim milk
1/2 cup finely diced green pepper (Optional)

Yield:	8 servings
Calories:	441
Fat:	1 g
Cholesterol:	6 mg
Sodium:	113 mg
Dietary Exchanges:....	4 Bread/Cereal

Spray crockpot with cooking spray (fat-free). Put all
ingredients into the crockpot. Mix. Cover. Cook at
low for 4 hours. Add milk if mixture becomes dry.

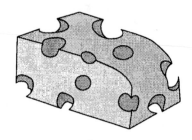

HEARTY BEEF STEW

2 lbs. stew beef, cut in 1 inch cubes
5 carrots, cut in 1 inch pieces
1 lg. onion, cut in chunks
3 stalks celery, sliced
1 (1 lb. 12 oz.) can tomatoes
1/2 cup quick-cooking tapioca
1 whole clove (or 1/2 tsp. ground cloves)
2 bay leaves
Salt and pepper to taste

Trim all fat from meat. Put all ingredients in the crock pot. Mix thoroughly. Cover and cook on low 12 hours (High: 5 to 6 hours).

Yield: .... 6 servings
Calories: 368
Fat: .... 12 g
Cholesterol: .... 125 mg
Sodium: .... 147 mg
Dietary Exchanges:.... 1 Bread
2 Vegetables
2 Medium-Fat Meats

JEAN'S POT ROAST OF BEEF

3 lbs. beef round steak, fat trimmed
3 potatoes, pared and sliced
2 to 3 carrots, pared and sliced
1 to 2 onions, peeled and sliced
1/2 cup water
Salt and pepper to taste

Put vegetables in bottom of crock pot. Salt and pepper meat, then put in pot. Add liquid. Cover and cook on low for 10 to 12 hours (High: 4 to 5 hours). Remove meat and vegetables with spatula.

Yield: .... 8 servings
Calories: 359
Fat: .... 13.8 g
Cholesterol: .... 140 mg
Sodium: .... 149 mg
Dietary Exchanges:.... 1 Vegetable
                         5 Meat
                         2 Fat

Jean Nelson

SHEPHERD'S PIE

6 med. potatoes, peeled and cooked
6 Tbsp. skim milk
Freshly ground white pepper, to taste
1 lb. turkey (or 2 cups chopped cooked meats)
2 tomatoes, peeled and chopped
Sm. bunch parsley, finely chopped
1 cup thinly sliced carrots, cooked
1 cup frozen sm. peas
1 cup low-salt mushroom gravy
1 tsp. Worcestershire sauce
Pinch of garlic powder

Puree potatoes and whip with milk, salt and pepper. Brown meat lightly in skillet (if not cooked); drain off fat. Add tomatoes, parsley, carrots, unthawed peas, gravy, Worcestershire sauce and garlic powder and mix together gently. Turn into crock. Spoon potatoes over top, swirling to cover. Cover. Bake 2 hours on high or 4 hours on low. Serve from crock.

Yield: .... 8 servings
Calories: 121
Fat: .... 8.4 g
Cholesterol: .... 27.2 mg
Sodium: .... 235 mg
Dietary Exchanges:.... 2 Vegetables
                         1 Lean Meat

TUNA NOODLE CASSEROLE

> 1 (8 or 10 oz.) pkg. Pasta Growers noodles, cooked and drained
> 1 (10 oz.) can condensed cream of celery soup*
> 2/3 cup skim milk
> 1 (1 lb.) pkg. frozen mixed vegetables, thawed
> 2 Tbsp. parsley flakes
> 2 (7 oz.) cans water-packed tuna
> 2 tsp. margarine, melted (Optional)

In a large bowl, combine soup, milk and vegetables, parsley flakes and tuna. Fold in cooked noodles and spray crock pot with non-stick spray. Pour ingredients into crock pot. Top with melted margarine (Optional). Cover and cook on low for 8 hours (High: 3 to 4 hours). If casserole appears dry, add 1/3 cup skim milk.

Yield:	8 servings
Calories:	227
Fat:	3 g
Cholesterol:	27 mg
Sodium:	453 mg
Dietary Exchanges:....	2 Bread/Starch
	1 Lean Meat

*To reduce fat and sodium, use 98% fat-free and reduced sodium and low cholesterol cream soups or homemade cream soup mix.

AUNT CAROLYN'S HAMBURGER SOUP

3 Tbsp. lowfat margarine
1 med. onion, chopped
1-1/2 lbs. lean ground beef
1 can (28 oz.) tomatoes
2 cans low-sodium beef consomme
2 soup cans water
4 carrots, sliced
4 celery tops, chopped
Parsley to taste
1-1/2 tsp. thyme
10 peppercorns
1/2 cup barley

Saute onions in margarine. Add beef, brown and drain. Add all other ingredients. Simmer (covered) for an hour or more.

Yield: .... 8 servings
Calories: 371
Fat: .... 14.5 g
Cholesterol: .... 98.8 mg
Sodium: .... 313 mg
Dietary Exchanges:.... 1 Vegetable
4 Medium-Fat Meat

BEAN SOUP PROVENCALE

1-1/2 cups chopped celery
1 cup sliced onion
1 cup sliced leeks
1/4 cup vegetable oil
8 cups water
1 cup sliced carrots
1 diced turnip
1 tsp. salt (Optional)
1/4 tsp. pepper
2 cans (16 oz.) Great Northern, sm. white
   or colored beans*
1 sm. sliced zucchini
1 cup sliced fresh or frozen chopped spinach
Pistou sauce

Saute celery, onion and leeks in oil about 10 minutes or until tender. Add water, carrots, turnip, salt and pepper. Bring to a boil; reduce heat, simmer 30 minutes or until vegetables are tender. Add beans, zucchini, spinach and heat thoroughly. Add 2 tsp. pistou sauce to soup and pass the remaining sauce.

Yield:	8 servings
Calories:	221
Fat:	7.47 g
Cholesterol:	0 mg
Sodium:	35.7 mg
Dietary Exchanges:	1 Bread
	2 Vegetables
	1 Fat

*3-1/3 cups drained, cooked beans can be substituted.

Karen Stensrud
Dakota Medical Center

CONDENSED CREAM SOUP MIX

Use as a casserole sauce mix or as a base for cream soups such as mushroom, asparagus, broccoli, cauliflower, etc. A can of Cream of Potato Soup contains 1860 mg sodium while our equivalent contains 152 mg sodium.

 2 cups non-fat dry milk powder
 3/4 cup cornstarch
 1/4 cup sodium-reduced, chicken-flavored
  bouillon granules
 2 Tbsp. dried onion flakes
 1 tsp. dried basil, crushed
 1 tsp. whole thyme
 1/2 tsp. pepper

Mix dry milk, cornstarch, bouillon granules, onion flakes, basil, thyme and pepper. Store in an airtight container.

To substitute for one can condensed soup, combine 1/3 cup dry mix with 1-1/4 cups water. Heat to boiling and cook and stir until thickened.

Yield: .... 9 (1/3 cup dry) servings
Calories: 156
Fat: .... .9 g
Cholesterol: .... 5 mg
Sodium: .... 152 mg
Dietary Exchanges:.... 1 Starch
 1 Skim Milk

HEARTY BEAN AND PASTA SOUP

3-1/2 cups water
1/2 cup uncooked Pasta Growers elbow spaghetti
   or small ditalini pasta
1/2 cup chopped celery
1 (9 oz.) pkg. frozen baby lima beans or
   8 oz. can butter beans, undrained*
1/2 cup chopped onion
1 tsp. dried basil leaves
1/2 tsp. salt
1/2 tsp. dried thyme leaves
1/4 to 1/2 tsp. crushed red pepper flakes,
   if desired
1 (16 oz.) can (2 cups) pork and beans, undrained
1 (16 oz.) can (2 cups) whole tomatoes, undrained,
   cut up, or 2 cups peeled, chopped tomatoes

Bring water to a boil in large saucepan or Dutch oven.
Stir in pasta, celery, lima beans, onion, basil, salt, thyme
and red pepper flakes. Return to a boil. Reduce heat;
simmer 7 to 10 minutes or until pasta is of desired
doneness. Stir in pork and beans and tomatoes; cook
until thoroughly heated. Garnish with shredded cheese,
if desired.

TIP: *If substituting 8 oz. can butter beans for frozen
lima beans, add with pork and beans.

Yield: .... 5 (1-1/2 cup) servings
Calories: 200
Fat: .... 2 g
Cholesterol: .... 1 mg
Sodium: .... 690 mg
Dietary Exchanges: .... 2 Starch
                                      2 Vegetable

LIGHT CHICKEN WILD RICE SOUP

    2 (14-1/2 oz.) cans ready-to-serve chicken
        broth with 1/3 less salt
    3 boneless, skinless chicken breast halves,
        cut into 3/4 inch cubes
    1 (6.25 oz.) pkg. quick-cooking long grain and
        wild rice mix (with seasoning packet)
    4 cups skim milk
    3/4 cup all purpose flour
    4 slices bacon, crisply cooked, crumbled
    1-1/2 tsp. diced pimiento
    1 Tbsp. dry sherry, if desired

In Dutch oven or large saucepan, combine broth, chicken, rice and seasoning packet; mix well. Bring to a boil. Reduce heat; cover and simmer 5 to 10 minutes or until rice is tender.

Lightly spoon flour into measuring cup; level off. In jar or container with tight-fitting lid, combine 1 cup of the milk and flour; shake until well blended. Add flour mixture, remaining milk, bacon, pimiento and sherry to rice mixture; cook and stir over medium heat until thickened and bubbly and chicken is no longer pink.

Yield: .... 6 (1-1/2 cup) servings
Calories: 330
Fat: .... 5 g
Cholesterol: .... 43 mg
Sodium: .... 1120 mg
Dietary Exchanges: .... 3 Starch
                                         2 Lean Meat

Desserts

APPLE CAKE

2/3 cup vegetable oil
1/2 cup sugar
4 egg whites
1 tsp. vanilla
1/2 tsp. baking soda
1 tsp. baking powder
1/2 tsp. cinnamon
1 cup all-purpose flour
1/2 whole wheat flour
2 cups diced apples

In a large bowl, mix oil, sugar, egg, vanilla, baking soda, baking powder, cinnamon, flour and apples. Pour into a non-stick sprayed 9x9 inch pan. Bake in 350° F oven for 30 minutes. Or may microwave.

Yield: .... 6 servings
Calories: 323
Fat: .... 12.6 g
Cholesterol: .... 0 mg
Sodium: .... 158 mg
Dietary Exchanges:..... 1 Bread
2 Fruit
2 Fat

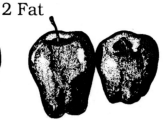

APPLE CRISP

6 cups sliced, peeled apples
1 tsp. cinnamon
1 tsp. water
1 tsp. lemon juice
1 cup rolled oats
3/4 cup all purpose flour
3/4 cup firmly packed brown sugar
1/2 cup low fat margarine, softened

Heat oven to 375° F. Place apples in ungreased 2-quart casserole. Sprinkle with cinnamon, water and lemon juice. In large bowl, combine remaining ingredients, mix with pastry blender or fork until crumbly. Sprinkle crumb mixture evenly over apples. Bake for 25-35 minutes or until fruit is tender and topping is golden brown.

Yield: .... 12 servings
Calories: 170
Fat: .... 4.40 g
Cholesterol: .... 0 mg
Sodium: .... 8 mg
Dietary Exchanges:..... 2 Fruit

Carrie Johnson,
Dakota Medical Center

CHOCOLATE CAKE

1 cup bran cereal
1 cup water
Dry sugar substitute equal to
   1/3 cup sugar (optional)
1 med. egg
1/4 cup canola oil
1 tsp. vanilla
1 tsp. of chocolate flavoring
1 Tbsp. lemon juice
1 cup all-purpose flour
1 tsp. soda
1/4 cup cocoa
1/4 cup sugar
2 Tbsp. instant dry milk
1/2 tsp. cinnamon
1/2 tsp. salt

Place bran, water, sugar, substitute, egg, vegetable oil, vanilla, chocolate flavoring and lemon juice in a mixer bowl.
Mix lightly and let stand for 30 -45 minutes. Combine flour,
soda, cocoa, sugar, dry milk, cinnamon and salt and stir to
blend well. Add flour mixture to the bran mixture and mix a
medium speed about 1/2 minute or until well blended. Place
in a well-greased 9-inch square cake pan and bake at 350° F
for about 20 minutes or until the cake springs back when
touched in the center and the sides of the cake pull away
from the sides of the pan. Cool to room temperature and cut
3 x 4 to yield 12 squares. Use 1 square per serving.

NOTE: This batter also makes excellent cupcakes. Spoon batter
into 12 muffin tins that have been sprayed with pan spray or
lined with paper liners and bake at 375° F for 15 to 20 minutes or until the cake springs back when touched in the center. The food exchanges will be the same for 1 cup-cake as for
1 piece of cake.

Yield: .... 1 9-inch cake (12 servings)
Calories: 119
Fat: .... 6 g
Cholesterol: .... 16 mg
Sodium: .... 224 mg
Dietary Exchanges: .... 1 Bread
                                      1 Fat
LOW-SODIUM DIETS: Omit salt.
LOW-CHOLESTEROL DIETS: Omit egg. Use 1/4 cup liquid
egg substitute.

CHOCOLATE POTATO CAKE

Cake:
1 (18.5 oz.) pkg. lowfat devil's food cake mix
3/4 cup mashed potato flakes
2 cups water
2 eggs

Filling:
1/4 cup apricot preserves

Chocolate Glaze:	or
1 cup powdered sugar	use Fat Free
1/4 cup chocolate syrup	Chocolate Fudge
1 tsp. vanilla	Topping

Heat oven to 350° F. Grease and flour two 9-inch round cake pans. In large bowl, combine all cake ingredients at low speed until moistened; beat 2 minutes at high speed. Pour into greased and floured pans. Bake at 350° F for 23 to 28 minutes or until toothpick inserted in center comes out clean. Cool 5 minutes; remove from pans. Cool completely.

Melt apricot preserves in small saucepan over low heat. Place 1 cake layer on serving platter; spread with melted preserves. Top with remaining layer.

In small bowl, combine all glaze ingredients until smooth. If needed, stir in water a few drops at a time for desired glaze consistency. Spoon glaze over cooled cake, allowing some to run down sides.

HIGH ALTITUDE: Above 3500 Feet; Add 1/4 cup flour to dry cake mix. Bake as directed.

Yield:	16 servings
Calories:	190
Fat:	3 g
Cholesterol:	28 mg
Sodium:	290 mg
Dietary Exchanges:	1 Starch
	1-1/2 Fruit
	1/2 Fat

CREAM CHEESE DESSERT

1 tub (12 oz.) light cream cheese product (room temperature)
1 lg. box (1.4 oz.) sugar-free vanilla instant pudding
3 cup skim milk
1 can (20 oz.) Lite Cherry Filling*

In small mixing bowl, combine pudding mix and milk. Beat on low speed to mix ingredients. Add cream cheese. Increase speed and beat until smooth and thickened. Pour into individual or large serving dish. Top with pie filling, and refrigerate.

Yield: .... 8 (1/2 cup) servings
Calories: 200
Fat: .... 7 g
Cholesterol: .... 24 mg
Sodium: .... 554 mg
Dietary Exchanges:..... 1 Starch
                          1/2 Milk
                          1-1/2 Fat

* The cherry filling contains sugar and should be limited by people with diabetes.

NO-CHOLESTEROL APPLE CAKE

Nonstick spray coating
2/3 cup sugar
1/2 cup packed brown sugar
1/4 cup vegetable oil
3 egg whites
2/3 cup all-purpose flour
2/3 cup whole wheat flour
1/2 cup oat bran
1-1/2 tsp. baking soda
1 tsp. ground cinnamon
1/4 tsp. ground allspice *or* nutmeg
3 cups shredded unpeeled apples
   Powdered sugar (optional)

Spray a 13x9x2 inch baking pan with nonstick coating; set aside. Combine sugar, brown sugar, oil, and egg whites in a large mixing bowl. Beat with a wooden spoon until well blended. Add all-purpose flour, whole wheat flour, oat bran, baking soda, cinnamon, and allspice or nutmeg; stir just until moistened. Stir in shredded apples. Pour batter into prepared pan. Bake in a 350° F for 25 to 30 minutes. Cool. If desired, sift powdered sugar atop cake.

Yield: .... 16 servings
Calories: 143
Fat: .... 4 g
Cholesterol: .... 0 mg
Sodium: .... 90 mg
Dietary Exchanges:..... 1-1/2 Bread
                           1/2 Fat

Rocky Hadrava, MS, LRD, Dakota Medical Center

OAT BRAN CRUNCHIES

1/2 cup margarine
1/2 cup brown sugar
1 Tbsp. water
1 tsp. vanilla
1 egg or 1/4 cup Liquid Egg Substitute
1/2 cup flour
1/4 cup whole wheat flour
1/2 tsp. baking soda
1/4 tsp. salt
3/4 cup oatmeal
3/4 cup oatflake cereal,
   lightly crushed
1/4 cup oat bran
2 Tbsp. sugar
1 tsp. cinnamon

Preheat oven to 350° F. Cream margarine and sugar with electric mixer until well blended. Add water, vanilla, and egg, beating well. Combine flours, soda, and salt and add to creamed mixture. Add oatmeal, oat flake cereal, and oat bran. Drop dough by spoonfuls onto a no-stick baking sheet. Combine 2 Tbsp. sugar and 1 tsp. cinnamon in a small bowl. Dip flat bottom of a glass into the sugar and cinnamon mixture and use to press dough flat. Bake for 7 minutes until browned. Cool on a wire rack. Store in covered container when cooled.

Yield: .... 30 cookies
Calories: 80
Fat: .... 4 g
Cholesterol: .... 9 mg
Sodium: .... 70 mg
Dietary Exchanges:..... 1/2 Starch/Bread
                              1 Fat
Preparation Time: .... 30 min.

PIE CRUST FOR
ALL SEASONS

3 egg whites at room temperature
1 cup sugar
1-1/2 tsp. vanilla
14 sq. soda crackers, rolled fine
1/2 tsp. baking soda
1/2 cup chopped walnuts

Preheat oven to 325° F. In a medium mixing bowl, beat egg white until frothy. Gradually add sugar until stiff peaks form. Fold in vanilla, crackers, soda, and nuts. Spray a 9-inch pie pan with nonstick cooking spray and transfer egg white mixture to the pan, spreading evenly over the bottom and sides. Bake for 45 minutes. Cool to room temperature and fill with fruit filling or skim milk based puddings.

Yield:	8 servings
Calories:	143
Fat:	3 g
Cholesterol:	0 mg
Sodium:	129 mg
Dietary Exchanges:.....	2 Bread/Starch
Preparation Time:	55 min.

RHUBARB CAKE

1-1/4 cups brown sugar
1/2 cup margarine
2 egg whites or 1 egg
1 tsp. vanilla
1-1/2 cups all-purpose flour
1/2 cup whole-wheat flour
1 cup buttermilk or sour skim milk*
1 tsp. soda
2-1/2 cups rhubarb, cut into 1/2" pieces

Topping:
1/4 cup sugar
2-1/2 tsp. cinnamon
1/2 cup chopped walnuts (optional)

*To make sour milk, place 1 Tbsp. lemon juice or vinegar in measuring cup and add milk to make 1 cup. In mixing bowl, cream brown sugar and margarine. Add egg whites or egg and beat. Add vanilla, flours, buttermilk or sour milk, and soda. Beat until smooth. Fold in rhubarb. Spread in a non-stick sprayed 9x13" pan. Mix sugar, cinnamon and walnuts and sprinkle over the batter. Bake at 350° F for 35 to 40 minutes . Serve warm or cold.

Yield: .... 24 pieces
Calories: 187
Fat: .... 6.3 g
Cholesterol: .... 0 mg
Sodium: .... 56 mg
Dietary Exchanges:..... 1 Starch
                                      1 Fruit
                                      1 Fat

STRAWBERRY TRIFLE

1/2 lg. or 1 sm. angel food cake
1 (3 oz.) box sugar-free strawberry gelatin
10 oz. no-sugar-added frozen strawberries,
    thawed
2 lg. bananas
2 (0.8 oz. or 0.9 oz.) boxes sugar-free instant
    reduced-calorie pudding & pie filling
9 oz. lite whipped topping
1 3/4 cups skim milk (mix with pudding)

Tear cake into bite-size pieces and place in bottom of
ungreased 9" x 13" pan. Dissolve gelatin in 1 cup boiling
water. Add strawberries and their juice to gelatin. Spoon
evenly over cake pieces. Slice bananas on top and
refrigerate. Prepare pudding with 1 3/4 cups skim milk.
Pour pudding over bananas and top with whipped topping.
Refrigerate 1 to 2 hours. Cut into squares. Garnish with
a slice of fresh strawberry.

Yield: .... 15 servings
Calories: 124
Fat: .... 3 g
Sodium: .... 315 mg
Dietary Exchanges:..... 1 Starch
                          1/2 Fruit
                          1/2 Fat

ZUCCHINI BROWNIES

3 cups peeled and grated zucchini
1-1/2 cups sugar
2/3 cup oil
3 cups flour
1/2 tsp. salt
2 tsp. soda
1/3 cup cocoa
3 tsp. vanilla
1/3 cup coconut
1/2 cup chopped almonds

Preheat oven to 350° F. Mix all ingredients together in 2-qt. mixing bowl. Spray an 8x15-inch pan with nonstick cooking spray. Spread batter in pan. Bake for 25 minutes or until toothpick inserted in center comes out clean. Dust with powdered sugar when cooled.

Yield: .... 30 (2-inch square) brownies
Calories: 137
Fat: .... 6 gm
Cholesterol: 0
Sodium: .... 92 mg
Dietary Exchanges:..... 1 Bread/Starch
                         1 Fat
Preparation Time: .... 45 minutes

NUTRITION ALERT: This recipe contains a significant amount of sugar, and may not be a good choice for insulin-dependent diabetics. Check with your dietitian if you have questions.

Especially For Kids, Pizza, Sandwiches & Snacks

BREAKFAST IN AN ENVELOPE

Fold a tortilla around a filling to make a fun finger breakfast. If you put out the fillings and the warm tortillas, children can make their own envelopes. Use your imagination to come up with new fillings children will enjoy.

Envelope fillings might include:
>   broccoli and cheese
>   peanut butter and raisins
>   cottage cheese and pineapple
>   bananas and finely chopped nuts
>   beans and cheese
>   scrambled eggs and green peppers
>   melon or berries and yogurt
>   carrot and raisin salad
>   cooked cauliflower and mild salsa
>   cooked cinnamon apples

Serve "envelopes" with milk and juice to make a complete breakfast.

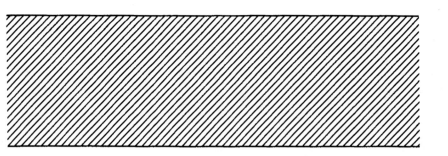

CHOCOLATE SMUNCHIES

1 pkg. sugar-free chocolate pudding mix
2 cups nonfat milk
3 cups peanut butter
70 graham cracker squares

Mix chocolate pudding according to directions on package using nonfat milk. Cool thoroughly. Mix peanut butter with pudding. Drop 1 Tbsp. onto 1 square graham cracker. Place low-calorie whipped topping on top of the pudding-peanut butter mixture, cover with second graham cracker square. Freeze until ready to use.

Yield: .... 35 (1 smunchie) servings
Calories: 200
Fat: .... 12 g
Sodium: .... 142 mg
Dietary Exchanges:.... 1 Starch/Bread
1 Medium-Fat Meat
1 Fat

MICROWAVE CHICKEN NUGGETS

1/4 cup flour
1/4 cup cornmeal
1 tsp. chili powder
1 tsp. paprika
1/2 tsp. garlic powder
1/8 to 1/4 tsp. cayenne pepper
1 egg white
2 (7 oz.) pkgs. boneless skinless chicken breast chunks*
1 cup mild salsa

Microwave Directions: In a paper or plastic bag, combine flour, cornmeal, chili powder, paprika, garlic powder and cayenne pepper. In shallow dish, beat egg white lightly with fork. Dip chicken pieces in egg white. Shake dipped chicken, 3 or 4 pieces at a time, in coating mixture. Place half of chicken pieces in circle around edge of microwave-safe waxed paper.

Microwave on high for 3 to 3-1/2 minutes or until chicken is no longer pink, turning chicken pieces once halfway through cooking. Repeat with remaining chicken pieces. Serve with salsa.

TIP: *One pound boneless skinless chicken breasts, cut into 1-1/2 inch pieces, can be substituted.

Yield: .... 4 (5 nugget) servings
Calories: 210
Fat: .... 3 g
Cholesterol: .... 62 mg
Sodium:........................ 530 mg
Dietary Exchanges:....... 1 Starch
                              2-1/2 Lean Meat

ORANGE SLUSH

1 (12 oz.) can frozen orange juice
1/2 cup sugar
1 cup milk
8 to 10 ice cubes

Combine all ingredients in a blender.

Yield: .... 6 servings
Calories: 165
Fat: .... .19 g
Cholesterol: .... .74 mg
Sodium: .... 22 mg
Dietary Exchanges:.... 1 Bread
                         1 Fruit
                         1 Milk

PURPLE COW

1 (12 oz.) can frozen grape juice
2 cups ice milk
2 cups skim milk

Combine ingredients in blender.

Yield: .... 6 servings
Calories: 124
Fat: .... 2 g
Cholesterol: .... 7.54 mg
Sodium: .... 79 mg
Dietary Exchanges:.... 1 Bread/Starch

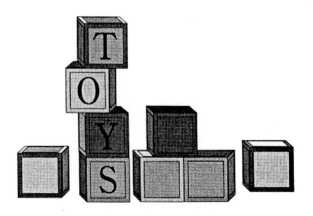

Gloria Olson
Dakota Medical Center

QUICK PEANUT BUTTER BALLS

3/4 cup graham cracker crumbs
  (about 12 squares)
1/3 cup dried currants or chopped raisins
1/3 cup peanut butter
2 Tbsp. applesauce
2 Tbsp. graham cracker crumbs (2 squares)

In small bowl, combine all ingredients except 2 Tbsp.
graham cracker crumbs; mix well. Shape mixture
into 3/4 inch balls. Roll in 2 Tbsp. graham cracker
crumbs. Store in refrigerator.

Yield:	22 (1 cookie) servings
Calories:	45
Fat:	2 g
Cholesterol:	0 mg
Sodium:	40 mg
Dietary Exchanges:....	1/2 Starch

SOFT PRETZELS

Children love to help make these!

1 loaf frozen bread dough
Poppy or sesame seeds

Cover dough and thaw overnight in refrigerator or for several hours at room temperature until soft enough to shape.

On a floured surface, cut dough the long way into 8 strips. Cover and let rise 10 minutes.

Roll each strip on floured surface until 1/2" thick and 18-20" long. Cut each strip in half and twist into pretzel shape. Place on a non-stick sprayed baking sheet. Brush with lukewarm water. Sprinkle with poppy or sesame seeds.

Let rise, uncovered, for 15 to 20 minutes. Place a shallow pan of hot water on bottom shelf of preheated oven. Bake pretzels at 425° F on middle shelf for 10 to 15 minutes.

Yield:	16 (1 pretzel) servings
Calories:	117
Fat:	2 g
Cholesterol:	0 mg
Sodium:	200 mg
Dietary Exchanges:....	1 Starch
	1/2 Fat

TUNA SALAD CONES

2-1/2 oz. (1/2 cup) uncooked macaroni rings
1/4 cup reduced-calorie mayonnaise
   or salad dressing
1/4 cup nonfat sour cream
1 to 2 Tbsp. skim milk
1 cup frozen sweet peas, thawed, drained
1 (6-1/8 oz.) can water-packed tuna,
   drained, flaked
1/8 tsp. salt
Dash pepper
8 flat-bottomed ice cream cones
1 oz. (1/4 cup) finely shredded reduced
   fat Cheddar cheese, if desired

Cook macaroni to desired doneness as directed on package. Drain; rinse with cool water. In medium bowl, combine all ingredients except ice cream cones and cheese; mix well. Cover; refrigerate until serving time.

To serve, fill each ice cream cone with generous 1/3 cup tuna salad. Top with cheese.

Yield:	8 (1 cone) servings
Calories:	150
Fat:	4 g
Cholesterol:	10 mg
Sodium:	220 mg
Dietary Exchanges:....	1 Starch
	1 Lean Meat

VEGETABLE CHICKEN TACOS

2 cups frozen broccoli, cauliflower and carrots, thawed, drained
1/2 cup mild salsa
1 (8 oz.) can kidney beans, drained
1 (5 oz.) can chunk chicken packed in water, drained
6 taco shells
6 Tbsp. shredded Cheddar cheese

Microwave Directions: In large microwave-safe bowl, combine all ingredients except taco shells and cheese. Microwave on high for 2 to 3 minutes or until thoroughly heated, stirring once halfway through cooking. Keep warm. Heat taco shells in microwave oven as directed on package.

Spoon vegetable mixture into taco shells; top with cheese.

Yield: .... 6 (1 taco) servings
Calories: 150
Fat: .... 6 g
Cholesterol: .... 28 mg
Sodium: .... 410 mg
Dietary Exchanges:.... 1 Starch
1 Medium-Fat Meat

DEEP DISH PIZZA

1 lb. loaf frozen white or wheat bread dough
1 Tbsp. vegetable oil (canola or olive)
8 oz. part-skim mozzarella cheese, shredded
8 oz. lean ground pork, browned
1/2 cup each chopped onion and green pepper
8 oz. no added salt tomato sauce
1/2 tsp. each garlic powder and fennel
1/4 tsp. pepper
1 tsp. each basil and oregano
1/2 tsp. sugar

Thaw frozen dough the day before in the refrigerator or oven-thaw. (To oven-thaw, preheat the oven to 200° F. Turn off oven. Place oiled bread dough in oiled 15x8-inch or 12-inch round pan. Cover with a towel and leave for 45 minutes in the preheated oven.) Work thawed dough to the edges and part way up the sides of the pan. Sprinkle first with cheese, then pork, onions, and pepper. Combine tomato sauce with seasonings and pour over all. Bake at 450° F for 40 minutes or until edges are browned and the middle has risen. Remove from the oven and allow to stand for 10 minutes. Cut and serve. Freeze or refrigerate leftovers.

Yield:	12 (1 slice) servings
Calories:	229
Fat:	10 g
Cholesterol:	22 mg
Sodium:	293 mg
Dietary Exchanges:	1-1/2 Bread/Starch
	2 Lean Meat
	1 Fat
Preparation Time:	60 minutes

FRENCH BREAD VEGGIE PIZZA

1 (12 inch) loaf French bread, halved lengthwise
1 (8 oz.) can pizza sauce
4 oz. (1 cup) shredded reduced-fat Cheddar cheese
1-1/2 cups seasoning blend of frozen onion,
    celery, sweet green and red peppers and
    parsley (from 10-oz. pkg.)*

Place French bread halves, cut side up, on ungreased broiler pan. Broil 4 to 6 inches from heat for 1 to 2 minutes or until light golden brown. Heat oven to 425° F. Spread pizza sauce over cut sides of bread. Sprinkle with half of cheese. Top with frozen vegetables. Bake for 10 minutes. Sprinkle with remaining cheese. Bake an additional 3 to 6 minutes or until cheese is melted.

TIP: *The seasoning blend is available in the frozen vegetable section of most supermarkets. You can make your own seasoning blend of vegetables by finely chopping and freezing onions, celery, red and green bell peppers and parsley on a cookie sheet until firm. When firm, transfer to a plastic freezer bag or other container and scoop out as needed.

Yield: .... 4 servings
Calories: 310
Fat: .... 8 g
Cholesterol: .... 21 mg
Sodium:.......................... 870 mg
Dietary Exchanges:........ 2 Starch
                             2 Vegetable
                             1 Medium-Fat Meat
                             1/2 Fat

Nutrition Alert: This recipe is high in sodium. Substitute low salt pizza sauce to reduce sodium.

FRESH VEGETABLE PIZZA WEDGES

1 (10 oz.) can refrigerated pizza crust

Filling:
3/4 cup lowfat cottage cheese
4 oz. light cream cheese (Neufchatel)
1 tsp. dried dill weed
1/8 tsp. garlic powder

Vegetables:
1 med. tomato, chopped
1 cup chopped broccoli florets
1/4 cup sliced green onions
1/2 cup chopped yellow summer squash
1/2 cup chopped carrot

Heat oven to 425° F. Spray 12-inch pizza pan with nonstick cooking spray. Unroll dough and place in spray-coated pan; starting at center, press out with hands, forming 1/2 inch rim. Prick dough generously with fork. Bake for 12 to 14 minutes or until golden brown. Place in refrigerator or freezer until cool.

In blender container or food processor bowl with metal blade, combine all filling ingredients; blend or process until smooth. Spread over cooled crust. Sprinkle tomato on filling along edge of crust. Continue forming rings of vegetables using broccoli, onions, carrot and squash, covering all filling. Cut into wedges to serve.

Yield:	6 (1 wedge) servings
Calories:	200
Fat:	5 g
Cholesterol:	13 mg
Sodium:	460 mg
Dietary Exchanges:	1-1/2 Starch
	1 Vegetable
	1 Fat

SCRAMBLED EGG PIZZA

1 to 2 Tbsp. cornmeal
1 loaf frozen Italian or white bread dough,
    thawed to room temperature
8 eggs
1/2 cup skim milk
1 Tbsp. margarine
1 cup pizza sauce
1 (4 oz.) can mushroom pieces and stems, drained
1/2 cup chopped green bell pepper
6 oz. (1-1/2 cups) shredded low-moisture
    part-skim mozzarella cheese
2 strips bacon, crisply cooked, crumbled,
    or 1 Tbsp. bacon flavor bits

Heat oven to 450° F. Grease 15x10x1 inch baking pan or 14 inch pizza pan; sprinkle evenly with cornmeal. On lightly floured surface, pat or roll out dough to a 15x10 inch rectangle. Place in coated pan. Press dough up sides to form rim.

Bake for 5 minutes. Check crust for bubbles; prick bubbles gently with fork. Bake an additional 5 minutes.

Meanwhile, in large bowl beat eggs and milk until well blended. Melt margarine in large nonstick skillet. Add egg mixture; cook over medium heat, stirring occasionally, just until eggs are set but still glossy. Do not overcook.

Spread pizza sauce over partially baked crust. Top with scrambled eggs, mushrooms, bell pepper, cheese and bacon. Bake for 5 to 8 minutes or until cheese is melted.

Yield:	12 (1 slice) servings
Calories:	220
Fat:	9 g
Cholesterol:	151 mg
Sodium:	470 mg
Dietary Exchanges:	1 Starch
	1 Vegetable
	1 Medium-Fat Meat
	1 Fat

CHICKEN CRANBERRY OPEN-FACED SANDWICHES

1 cup prepared lowfat chicken salad*
2 Tbsp. frozen cranberry-orange relish,
   thawed**
8 thin slices rye or whole grain
   mini-party bread
3 Tbsp. fat-free mayonnaise
8 leaf lettuce leaves
4 seedless red grapes, halved

In small bowl, combine chicken salad and cranberry-orange relish. Spread each bread slice with about 1 tsp. mayonnaise; top with lettuce leaf. Spoon chicken mixture onto lettuce. Garnish with grape halves.

TIPS:* Lowfat chicken salad can be purchased in the deli department of some large supermarkets. If unavailable, prepare chicken salad using 1 cup chopped cooked chicken, 1/3 cup diced celery and 3 to 4 Tbsp. fat-free mayonnaise; mix well.

**Canned cranberry-orange relish can be substituted for the frozen relish.

Yield:	8 (1 sandwich) servings
Calories:	120
Fat:	2 g
Cholesterol:	17 mg
Sodium:	330 mg
Dietary Exchanges:	1 Starch
	1 Lean Meat

DENVER TORTILLA FOLD-UPS

2 (8 oz.) ctns. frozen fat-free egg substitute, thawed
1/2 tsp. salt
1/4 tsp. pepper
1 Tbsp. oil
1/2 cup chopped onion
1/2 cup chopped green bell pepper
4 (7 or 8 inch) flour tortillas
1/4 cup taco sauce
2 oz. (1/2 cup) shredded Cheddar cheese

In medium bowl, combine egg substitute, salt and pepper; beat until blended. Heat oil in large skillet over medium heat until it ripples. Add onion and green pepper; cook 4 minutes or until vegetables are tender, stirring occasionally. Stir in beaten egg mixture. Cook over medium heat for 3 to 4 minutes or until eggs are set but still shiny, stirring occasionally.

Meanwhile, heat another skillet over medium heat until drop of water sizzles. Heat tortillas 1 at a time, about 15 seconds, turning once. Spoon about 1/2 cup cooked egg mixture onto top half of each tortilla. Spoon taco sauce over eggs. Fold bottom half of tortilla over eggs. Fold in half again, forming a quarter circle with 2 pockets. Sprinkle cheese into each pocket.

Yield:	4 (1 sandwich) servings
Calories:	250
Fat:	11 g
Cholesterol:	17 mg
Sodium:	760 mg
Dietary Exchanges:	1 Starch
	1 Vegetable
	2-1/2 Lean Meat

Nutrition Alert: This recipe is high in sodium. To reduce sodium, omit salt and substitute a low sodium/salt taco sauce.

NUTTY TURKEY SANDWICH

1 tsp. sunflower nuts
Cream cheese
1 oz. thin sliced turkey
2 slices light rye bread
2 Tbsp. alfalfa sprouts (Optional)

Spread cream cheese on bread; sprinkle sunflower nuts on and layer turkey and alfalfa sprouts.

Yield: .... 1 serving
Calories: 191
Fat: .... 4 g
Cholesterol: .... 19.6 mg
Sodium: .... 368 mg
Dietary Exchanges: .... 1 Bread
                          1 Vegetable
                          1 Lean Meat

OPEN-FACED DENVER SANDWICHES

1 (8 oz.) ctn. (1 cup) frozen fat-free egg
   product, thawed, or 4 eggs, beaten
1/2 cup skim milk
1 tsp. onion powder
Dash pepper
1/2 cup chopped reduced-sodium lowfat ham
1/4 cup chopped green bell pepper
8 slices tomato
4 whole wheat English muffins, split, toasted

In medium bowl, combine egg product, milk, onion powder and pepper; mix well. Spray medium non-stick skillet with nonstick cooking spray; heat over medium heat until hot. Add ham and bell pepper; cook 1 to 2 minutes or until pepper is crisp-tender. Drain, if necessary. Add egg mixture to skillet. Cook over medium heat until set but still moist, stirring frequently. Place tomato slice on each toasted muffin half; top each with egg mixture.

Yield: .... 4 (2 sandwich) servings
Calories: 210
Fat: .... 2 g
Cholesterol: .... 9 mg
Sodium: .... 250 mg
Dietary Exchanges:.... 2 Starch
                                     1 Lean Meat

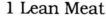

TURKEY FRENCH DIPS

    4 oz. cooked turkey slices
    4 (6 inch) French rolls
    4 oz. part-skim mozzarella cheese
    1 pkg. au jus gravy mix

Preheat oven to 400° F. Cut French rolls lengthwise. Place 1 oz. turkey and 1 oz. mozzarella cheese on each French roll. Wrap each roll in aluminum foil and heat in the oven for 10 minutes. Mix au jus according to package directions, or add more water to reduce the sodium content. Slice each sandwich in half, diagonally. Serve each with 1/3 cup au jus.

Yield:	4 (1 sandwich) servings
Calories:	355
Fat:	3 g
Cholesterol:	8 mg
Sodium:	485 mg
Dietary Exchanges:....	3 Starch
	2 Lean Meat

Variation: Omit cheese and use 2 oz. turkey.

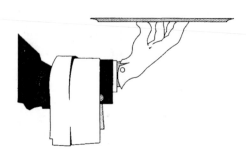

VEGGIE SANDWICH

2 slices whole wheat bread
Sunflower seeds
Sliced cucumbers
Sliced tomatoes
1 oz. American cheese
Alfalfa sprouts
Avocado dip

Spread avocado dip on bread; layer cucumbers, tomatoes, cheese and alfalfa sprouts.

Yield: .... 1 serving
Calories: 244
Fat: .... 10.7 g
Cholesterol: .... 27 mg
Sodium: .... 620 mg
Dietary Exchanges:.... 2 Bread
                             1 Medium-Fat Meat
                             1 Fat

Yvonne Erickson

WALK-AWAY SEAFOOD POCKETS

1/2 cup light sour cream
2 Tbsp. fat-free salad dressing
1 Tbsp. dried dill weed
1/2 tsp. dried tarragon leaves
1/2 tsp. lemon pepper seasoning
1 (8 oz.) pkg. imitation crab meat (surimi),
  coarsely chopped
1/2 cup thinly sliced green onions
1/2 cup thinly sliced celery
4 (6 inch) pocket (pita) breads

In large bowl, combine sour cream, salad dressing, dill weed, tarragon and lemon pepper seasoning; blend well. Add crab meat, onions and celery; toss well to coat. Cut each pocket bread into 2 pieces with 1 piece slightly smaller than the other. Carefully open larger piece; tuck smaller piece into larger piece. Open smaller piece, spoon generous 1/2 cup of filling into pocket. Repeat for remaining sandwiches.

Yield:	4 (1 sandwich) servings
Calories:	350
Fat:	4 g
Cholesterol:	24 mg
Sodium:	770 mg
Dietary Exchanges:....	3 Starch
	1 Vegetable
	2 Lean Meat

*Nutrition Alert: This recipe is high in sodium. It is intended to be used for occasional use only. Substitute rinsed water packed tuna in place of imitation crab meat to reduce sodium.

BAGEL PIZZA SNACKS

1 (6-oz.) can tomato paste
3/4 to 1 tsp. dried oregano leaves
5 whole wheat or white bagels, split
1/2 cup chopped green bell pepper,
    mushrooms or black olives
3 oz. (3/4 cup) shredded mozzarella cheese

Heat oven to 450° F. In small bowl, combine tomato paste and oregano. Spread each bagel half with about 1 Tbsp. tomato paste mixture. Place on ungreased cookie sheet. Top each with bell pepper; sprinkle with cheese. Bake for 6 to 8 minutes or until cheese is melted.

Yield: .... 10 servings
Calories: 120
Fat: .... 2 g
Cholesterol: .... 5 mg
Sodium: .... 280 mg
Dietary Exchanges:..... 1 Starch
                           1/2 Med-Fat Meat

CHOCOLATE POPCORN

6 cups popped popcorn
1 Tbsp. margarine
2 Tbsp. light corn syrup
1 Tbsp. cocoa powder
1-1/2 Tbsp. skim milk
1/8 tsp. salt

Keep popcorn warm in oven while making chocolate
sauce. In small pan, melt margarine over low heat.
Add corn syrup, cocoa, milk, and salt. Stir over low
heat until well blended and mixture is hot. Pour over
warm popcorn. Quickly stir to coat all pieces.

Yield: .... 6 (1 cup) servings
Calories: 94
Fat: .... 2 g
Cholesterol: .... 0 mg
Sodium: .... 82 mg
Dietary Exchanges: ..... 1 Starch/Bread

FANCY POPCORN TOSS

1/4 cup margarine, melted
1/4 tsp. garlic powder
1/4 tsp. onion powder
1/4 tsp. celery salt
2 tsp. Worcestershire sauce
5 drops Tabasco sauce
6 cups popped popcorn
1 cup chow mein noodles
1 cup pretzel sticks

Combine melted margarine with the next 5 ingredients. In large baking pan, mix together popcorn, chow mein noodles, and pretzels. Pour melted margarine and seasonings over popcorn mixture. Stir until well mixed. Bake at 275° for 45 minutes, stirring several times. Serve warm.

Yield: .... 8 (1 cup) servings
Calories: 240
Fat: .... 10 g
Cholesterol: .... 0 mg
Sodium: .... 696 mg
Dietary Exchanges:..... 2 Starch/Bread
                                         2 Fat

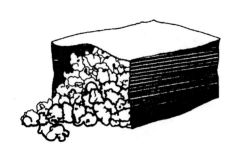

PINK PERFECT POPCORN

6 cups popped popcorn
2-1/2 Tbsp. margarine
1 tsp. sugar-free strawberry flavored gelatin

Keep popcorn warm in oven. In small saucepan over low heat, melt margarine. Cool slightly. Quickly stir in strawberry gelatin and immediately pour over popcorn tossing to coat all pieces.

Yield: .... 6 (1 cup servings)
Calories: 112
Fat: .... 6 g
Cholesterol: .... 0 mg
Sodium: .... 80 mg
Dietary Exchanges: 1 Starch/Bread
                                    1 Fat

Fruits, Vegetables & Salads

CITRUS MARINATED FRUIT

    1 cup fresh or frozen cantaloupe balls
    1 cup fresh or frozen blueberries
    1 cup halved green grapes
    1 cup fresh or frozen halved strawberries,
       unsweetened
    1 Tbsp. sugar
    3/4 cup orange juice
    1/4 cup dry white wine or white grape juice
    2 Tbsp. lemon juice
    Fresh mint leaves, if desired

In large bowl, combine cantaloupe, blueberries, grapes and strawberries. In small bowl, combine sugar, orange juice, wine and lemon juice; mix well. Pour over fruit. Cover; refrigerate 2 to 3 hours to blend flavors, stirring occasionally. To serve, spoon fruit and marinade into individual dishes. Garnish with mint leaves, if desired.

Yield: .... 8 (1/2 cup) servings
Calories: 60
Fat: .... 35 g
Cholesterol: .... 0 mg
Sodium: .... 5 mg
Dietary Exchanges:.... 1 Fruit

Jan Sliper, LRD
Robyn Vinje, MS, LRD
Kathy Tehven, LRD
Paula Anderson, LRD
Lorraine Hanna, LRD
Dakota Medical Center

FROZEN FRUIT SALAD

2 cups sugar
2 cups water
2 (6 oz.) cans frozen orange juice
1 (No. 2) can crushed pineapple
2 (No. 2) cans apricots
6 bananas, mashed
2 Tbsp. lemon juice

Dissolve sugar in hot water. Add frozen orange juice, not thawed. Add crushed pineapple and juice, cut up apricots and juice, mashed bananas and lemon juice; mix all together. Line muffin tins with paper cups; fill. Freeze; take out 20 minutes before serving.

Yield: .... 40 servings
Calories: 70
Fat: .... .11 g
Cholesterol: .... 0 mg
Sodium: .... 1 mg
Dietary Exchanges:.... 1 Fruit

FRESH FRUIT SOUP

3 Tbsp. minute tapioca
2 Tbsp. sugar or equivalent sugar substitute
1 cup water
6 oz. frozen orange juice concentrate
16 oz. frozen strawberries without sugar
1 sm. can mandarin oranges

Combine tapioca, sugar, and water in a saucepan and allow to stand for 5 minutes. Then cook until clear. (If using sugar substitute, add to tapioca after cooking.) Add orange juice, strawberries, and oranges. Chill for 30 minutes. This dessert keeps well covered and refrigerated for 3 days.

Yield: .... 8 (1 cup) servings
Calories: 132
Fat: .... less than 1 g
Cholesterol: .... 0 mg
Sodium: .... 4 mg
Dietary Exchanges:.... 2 Fruit
Preparation Time: ...... 45 minutes

FRUITED RICE PILAF

1 Tbsp. margarine
1 Tbsp. finely chopped onion
1 garlic clove, minced
1 cup uncooked long grain rice
1 (14-1/2 oz.) can 1/3-less-salt chicken broth
   (not condensed)
1/3 cup water
1/2 cup dried fruit bits
1/2 tsp. dried thyme leaves

Melt margarine in medium saucepan over medium-high heat. Add onion and garlic; cook and stir until vegetables are crisp-tender. Remove from heat; add rice and stir until coated. Stir in broth, water, fruit bits and thyme. Bring to a boil. Reduce heat, cover and simmer 15 to 20 minutes or until rice is tender and liquid is absorbed.

Yield:	5 (1/2 cup) servings
Calories:	200
Fat:	3 g
Cholesterol:	0 mg
Sodium:	320 mg
Dietary Exchanges:....	2 Starch
	1/2 Fruit
	1/2 Fat

FRUIT KABOBS

1 cup strawberries
1 cup pineapple chunks
1 cup mandarin oranges
1 cup green grapes
1 cup cantaloupe

Dip/Topping:
12 oz. fat-free cream cheese
Juice from pineapple packed in its own juice
3 Tbsp. marshmallow creme
1/2 tsp. nutmeg

Wash and prepare fruit for wooden skewers. Place strawberry, pineapple chunk, mandarin orange, green grapes, and cantaloupe on wooden skewer for each serving

DIP/DRESSING: Blend fat-free cream cheese, marshmallow creme and pineapple juice. Add nutmeg. Serve fruit skewer with dip. Suggest serving sandwich with this for a menu idea.

Yield:	8 servings
Calories:	77
Fat:	0 g
Cholesterol:	0 mg
Sodium:	9.97 mg
Dietary Exchanges:	1 Fruit

Geri Weeding
Dakota Medical Center

FRUITS IN WINE

2 cups fresh, canned or frozen fruit
2 Tbsp. white wine
2 Tbsp. sugar

Mix fruit, wine and sugar and serve.

Yield: .... 4 (1/2 cup) servings
Calories: 80
Fat: .... 0 g
Cholesterol: .... 0 gm
Sodium: .... 0 gm
Dietary Exchanges:.... 1-1/2 Fruit

SUPERFAST RECIPE

KIWI FOR COMPANY

6 kiwi fruits, peeled and sliced
8 oz. pineapple chunks, in juice
3 bananas, sliced diagonally

Dressing:
1-1/2 tsp. grated orange peel
1/2 tsp. ginger
1 cup nonfat yogurt
1/4 cup light mayonnaise
2 Tbsp. honey

In a large salad bowl, gently mix kiwi fruit, pine-apple and juice, bananas, and grapes. Cover and refrigerate for 20 minutes, allowing flavors to blend. Combine ingredients for dressing with a whisk in a small mixing bowl. Pour dressing over fruits just before serving. This dessert can be used as a left-over for up to 48 hours.

Yield: .... 8 (1 cup) servings
Calories: 153
Fat: .... 3 g
Cholesterol: .... 3 mg
Sodium: .... 45 mg
Dietary Exchanges:.... 2 Fruit
                         1 Fat
Preparation Time: ...... 30 minutes

PEACH PIZZAZ

2 (10 oz.) pkgs. frozen peach slices,
   partially thawed
6 oz. can frozen lemonade concentrate,
   partially thawed
2/3 cup water
12 ice cubes

In 5 cup blender container, combine peaches, lemonade concentrate and water. Cover; blend at medium-low speed 30 seconds. Add ice cubes, one at a time, blending at low speed until slushy. Pour into non-metal pitcher. If desired, garnish with peach or lemon slices.

Yield:	5 (1 cup) servings
Calories:	62
Fat:	.11 g
Cholesterol:	0 mg
Sodium:	1 mg
Dietary Exchanges:....	1 Fruit

SNAPPY BAKED FRUIT

1 (16 oz.) can sliced peaches, drained
1 (16 oz.) can pear halves, drained, chopped
1/2 teaspoon grated lemon peel, if desired
1 cup crushed gingersnap cookies (about 14)
1 Tbsp. margarine or butter, melted

Heat oven to 375° F. In medium bowl, combine peaches, pears and lemon peel; mix well. Divide fruit mixture evenly among six 6-oz. custard cups. In small bowl, combine crushed cookies and margarine; mix well. Sprinkle evenly over fruit. Bake for 12 to 15 minutes or until hot and bubbly.

Yield: .... 6 (1/2 cup) servings
Calories: 140
Fat: .... 4 g
Cholesterol: .... 7 mg
Sodium: .... 135 mg
Dietary Exchanges:.... 2 Fruit
1 Fat

SPICED FRUIT MOLD

1 cup apple juice or apple cider
4 inches stick cinnamon
4 whole cloves
1 env. unflavored gelatin
3/4 cup orange juice
1 apple, chopped
2/3 cup orange sections, chopped

In saucepan, combine 3/4 cup of the apple juice or cider, the cinnamon and cloves. Simmer, covered for 15 minutes; remove spices. Meanwhile, soften gelatin in the remaining 1/4 cup apple juice or cider. Add to apple juice in saucepan; cook and stir in orange juice. Chill until partially set. Fold apple and orange sections into gelatin mixture. Turn into 3-1/2 cup mold. Chill several hours or until firm. Unmold to serve.

Yield: .... 6 (1/2 cup) servings
Calories: 9
Fat: .... .02 g
Cholesterol: .... 0 g
Sodium: .... 0 g
Dietary Exchanges:.... 1 Fruit

APPLE-GLAZED CARROTS

1 (14-oz.) pkg. frozen baby carrots
    or 2 cups fresh baby carrots
1/4 cup unsweetened apple juice or
    apple cider
1/4 cup apple jelly
1-1/2 tsp. Dijon mustard

Place carrots and apple juice in medium nonstick skillet. Bring to a boil. Reduce heat; cover and simmer 7 to 9 minutes or until carrots are crisp-tender. Uncover; cook over medium heat until liquid evaporates. Stir in jelly and mustard; cook and stir over medium heat until jelly melts and carrots are glazed.

Yield: .... 4 (1/2 cup) servings
Calories: 90
Fat: .... 0 g
Cholesterol: .... 0 mg
Sodium: .... 85 mg
Dietary Exchanges:..... 1 Vegetable
                                        1 Fruit

BAKED CARROTS AND SPROUTS

2 Tbsp. liquid oil margarine
1/2 cup chopped onion
1/4 cup flour
1 tsp. dill weed
3 cups skim milk
1/3 cup chopped fresh parsley
2 cups fresh Brussels sprouts
3 cups sliced fresh carrots

Steam fresh sprouts and carrots with 2 Tbsp. water in a covered dish in the MICROWAVE for 5 minutes. Drain off water. Meanwhile, saute onion in margarine in a medium-sized skillet. Stir in flour and dill weed, then gradually stir in milk. Cook until thick. Pour sauce over vegetables, and top with fresh parsley. MICROWAVE FOR 12 minutes, uncovered, on high power or bake, uncovered, for 30 minutes at 350° F.

Yield:	8 (1 cup) servings
Calories:	108
Fat:	4 g
Cholesterol:	1 mg
Sodium:	227 mg
Dietary Exchanges:.....	1/2 Bread/Starch
	1 Vegetable
	1 Fat
Preparation Time:	20 min., if microwaved

BROILED ASPARAGUS MAIN DISH

1 lb. asparagus, cleaned, stemmed, and
   steamed until tender
8 oz. shredded part-skim farmer cheese
1 cup croutons

Clean, stem and steam asparagus until tender. Place
on broiler-proof pan and top with cheese and croutons. Broil until cheese bubbles.

Yield: .... 4 servings
Calories: 238
Fat: .... 10 g
Cholesterol: .... 30 mg
Sodium: .... 417 mg
Dietary Exchanges:..... 3 Vegetable
                          2 Lean Meat
                          1 Fat

* Superfast Recipe

CHICKEN-TOPPED POTATOES

4 potatoes
8 oz. cooked chicken pieces
5 oz. reduced sodium cream of celery soup
2 Tbsp. green chilis or scallions

Bake 4 potatoes. Lay the potato on its flat side and slice across it both ways, creating a middle cavity. Stuff with a mixture of: cooked chicken pieces, reduced fat/sodium cream of celery soup, green chilis or scallions. Cover and microwave for 3 minutes on high power.

Yield: .... 4 servings
Calories: 338
Fat: .... 4 g
Cholesterol: .... 44 mg
Sodium: .... 234 mg
Dietary Exchanges: ..... 3 Starch/Bread
                          2 Lean Meat

* Superfast Recipe

LEFTOVER VEGETABLE STIR-FRY

Combine the following in a no-stock skillet:

>   4 cups leftover steamed vegetables
>   2 cups drained canned chicken or salmon
>   2 tsp. dill weed
>   1 Tbsp. vegetable oil

Stir-fry until heated through.

Yield:	4 servings
Calories:	130
Fat:	5 g
Cholesterol:	44 mg
Sodium:	39 mg
Dietary Exchanges:.....	1 Vegetable
	2 Lean Meat

* Superfast Recipe

GERMAN RED CABBAGE

    1 head red cabbage
    1 cup water
    1/2 cup chopped onion
    1 small apple, chopped
    3 bay leaves
    1/4 cup vinegar
    2 Tbsp. brown sugar
    4 slices bacon, broiled crisp
      and crumbled

Coarsely shred cabbage and place in 3-qt. sauce
pan with water, onion, apple, and bay leaves. Bring
to a boil and cook for 12 to 15 minutes. Drain in
colander, removing bay leaves. Transfer to a serving
bowl and add vinegar, sugar, and bacon. Mix well
and serve immediately.

Yield: .... 8 (1 cup) servings
Calories: 92
Fat: .... 2 g
Cholesterol: .... 3 mg
Sodium: .... 70 mg
Dietary Exchanges:..... 2 Vegetable
                         1 Fat
Preparation Time: .... 20 min.

LEMON ZUCCHINI

4 small zucchini, peeled and
   sliced thin
2 Tbsp. water
2 Tbsp. chopped onion
1/3 cup parsley
1 Tbsp. margarine
1/2 tsp. grated lemon peel
2 Tbsp. lemon juice

In a covered dish, combine zucchini with water. Cover
and MICROWAVE on high power for 5 minutes.
Drain. Meanwhile, saute onion and parsley in margarine in a skillet. Stir in lemon peel and juice. Add
steamed zucchini to the pan and toss. Serve hot.

Yield: .... 4 (1 cup) servings
Calories: 36
Fat: .... 3 g
Cholesterol: .... 0 mg
Sodium: .... 1 mg
Dietary Exchanges:..... 1 Vegetable
                         1/2 Fat
Preparation Time: .... 15 min.

OLD-FASHIONED CUKES

2 cucumbers
1 onion
1 tsp. salt
1 tray ice cubes
1/4 cup sugar
1/2 cup vinegar

Slice 2 cucumbers and 1 onion in a shallow bowl and cover with 1 tsp. salt and 1 tray of ice cubes. Allow to sit for 30 minutes. Meanwhile mix 1/4 cup sugar and 1/2 cup vinegar. Drain vegetables and combine in a bowl with dressing. This will keep in the refrigerator for 3 days.

Yield: .... 4 servings
Calories: 72
Fat: .... 0 g
Cholesterol: .... 0 mg
Sodium: .... 0 mg
Dietary Exchanges:..... 1 Vegetable
                        1 Fruit

* Superfast Recipe

MICROWAVE CITRUS SQUASH

1 med. acorn or buttercup squash
1 Tbsp. brown sugar
1 Tbsp. margarine
1 Tbsp. maple syrup
3 Tbsp. orange juice
1/2 tsp. grated lemon or orange peel

MICROWAVE DIRECTIONS:

Cut squash lengthwise into quarters; remove seeds and fibers. Arrange squash in 12x8 inch (2-quart) microwave-safe dish.

In small microwave-safe bowl, combine remaining ingredients. Microwave on HIGH for 30 to 45 seconds or until margarine is melted; mix well. Spoon mixture onto each squash section, allowing excess to run over sides. Cover with microwave-safe plastic wrap. Microwave on HIGH for 10 to 12 minutes or until tender. To serve, spoon syrup mixture over squash sections.

Yield: .... 4 servings
Calories: 100
Fat: .... 3 g
Cholesterol: .... 0 mg
Sodium: .... 40 mg
Dietary Exchanges:..... 1/2 Starch
1/2 Fruit
1/2 Fat

PEA SALAD

1 cup each of thawed green peas,
   tomatoes, and celery
1/2 cup reduced-calorie
   1000 Island dressing

Mix 1 cup each of thawed green peas, tomatoes, and
celery with 1/2 cup reduced-calorie 1000 Island
dressing.

Yield: .... 4 servings
Calories: 89
Fat: .... 1 g
Cholesterol: .... 2 mg
Sodium: .... 322 mg
Dietary Exchanges:..... 1 Starch/Bread

* Superfast Recipe

SNAPPY STUFFED PEPPERS

Clean 4 peppers and remove seeds. Mix the following together and stuff the peppers:

>   1 cup quick rice
>   1/2 cup water
>   8 oz. no added salt tomato sauce
>   8 oz. shredded mozzarella cheese
>   2 tsp. basil

Cover stuffed peppers and microwave for 15 minutes on 50% power.

Yield: .... 4 servings
Calories: 300
Fat: .... 10 g
Cholesterol: .... 30 mg
Sodium: .... 629 mg
Dietary Exchanges:..... 2 Starch/Bread
                                  2 Lean Meat
                                  1 Vegetable

* Superfast Recipe

STUFFED SQUASH

1/2 cup raisins or finely chopped apples
2 Tbsp. brown sugar
2 halves of an acorn squash

Combine 1/2 cup raisins or finely chopped apples with 2 Tbsp. brown sugar. Stuff into 2 halves of an acorn squash. Place in a casserole dish, cover, and microwave for 12 to 15 minutes on high power.

Yield:	4 servings
Calories:	127
Fat:	less than 1 g
Cholesterol:	0 mg
Sodium:	5 mg
Dietary Exchanges:	2 Starch/Bread

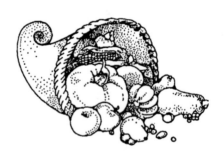

* Superfast Recipe

SUGAR AND SPROUTS

2 cups Brussels sprouts
2 tsp. lemon juice
2 Tbsp. brown sugar

Steam Brussels sprouts, dot with lemon juice and brown sugar.

Yield: .... 4 servings
Calories: 50
Fat: .... 0 g
Cholesterol: .... 0 mg
Sodium: .... 0 mg
Dietary Exchanges: ..... 2 Vegetable

* Superfast Recipe

RANCH BEANS

1/4 cup chopped green pepper
1 can (16 oz.) vegetarian baked beans
1 can (15 oz.) red kidney beans, drained
2 Tbsp. ketchup
2 Tbsp. molasses
1 Tbsp. Dijon mustard
1/2 tsp. dried onion

Stovetop Method: Place all ingredients in saucepan and heat thoroughly (about 10 minutes).

Microwave Method: Place all ingredients in a microwave safe bowl. Cover with wax paper, cook on high for 5 minutes, stirring halfway through cooking time.

Yield:	3 cups
	6 (1/2 cup servings)
Calories:	150
Fat:	1/2 g
Sodium:	594 mg
Dietary Exchanges:.....	2 Starch

REFRIED BEANS

Try this low fat version of refried beans.

      1 can (15 1/4 oz.) pinto beans, drained
      1/2 cup salsa

Drain beans. Spray pan with non-sticking coating. Add beans and mash. Add salsa and heat thoroughly.

Yield: .... 4 servings
Calories: 65
Fat: .... 0 g
Sodium: .... 282 mg
Dietary Exchanges:..... 1 Starch

ROASTED AUTUMN VEGETABLES

1/2 lbs. small red potatoes
1 Tbsp. olive oil
Bay leaf
1/4 tsp. dried thyme, crumbled
Garlic cloves, crushed
2 lbs. butternut squash, peeled and cut
   into 3/4 in. pieces - about 4 cups
Fresh thyme sprigs for garnish,
   if desired

In a bowl toss together the potatoes, quartered, 4 Tbsp. of the oil, bay leaf, dried thyme, garlic, and salt and pepper to taste. Spread the vegetables in an oiled large toasting pan and roast them in the middle of a preheated 375° oven, shaking pan every 5 to 10 minutes, for 25 minutes. In a bowl toss the squash with the remaining 1 Tbsp. oil and salt and pepper to taste and add it to the pan. Roast the vegetables, shaking the pan occasionally, for 10 to 20 minutes more, or until they are tender. Discard the bay leaf and garnish the vegetables with the thyme sprigs.

Yield:	8 servings
Calories:	172
Fat:	8.71 g
Cholesterol:	0 mg
Sodium:	176 mg
Dietary Exchanges:.....	1 Bread

SKILLET ACORN SQUASH

1 lg. (2-lb.) acorn squash
1/2 cup apple juice
1 Tbsp. margarine
1/4 tsp. cinnamon

Trim ends off squash. Stand squash on end; cut in half. Remove and discard seeds and fiber. Slice each squash half crosswise into 1/2-inch slices.

In 12-inch skillet, combine apple juice, margarine and cinnamon; mix well. Add squash. Bring to a boil. Reduce heat; cover and simmer 10 minutes. Turn slices; cover and simmer an additional 5 to 8 minutes or until squash is tender.

Yield: .... 4 servings
Calories: 100
Fat: .... 3 g
Cholesterol: .... 0 mg
Sodium: .... 40 mg
Dietary Exchanges:..... 1 Starch
                         1/2 Fat

SOUTHERN BEAN MEDLEY

1 (15-oz.) can black-eyed peas,
   drained, rinsed
1 (15.5-oz.) can lima beans,
   drained, rinsed
1 (15.5-oz.) can red beans or
   kidney beans, drained, rinsed
1 (14.5-oz.) can no-salt added stewed
   tomatoes, undrained, cut up
4 oz. turkey ham, cut into 1/2-inch cubes
1 tsp. dried basil leaves
1/2 tsp. dried thyme leaves, crushed
1/8 tsp. garlic powder
1/8 tsp. pepper
2 to 3 drops hot pepper sauce

Combine all ingredients in large saucepan; stir gently. Bring to a boil. Reduce heat; cover and simmer, stirring occasionally, until slightly thickened, about 15 minutes. If desired, garnish with fresh parsley or thyme.

Yield:	5 (1 cup) servings
Calories:	230
Fat:	2 g
Cholesterol:	17 mg
Sodium:	560 mg
Dietary Exchanges:.....	2 Starch
	1-1/2 Lean Meat

SPICED RED CABBAGE

4 cups shredded red cabbage
1/4 cup cider vinegar
1/2 cup water
1/4 tsp. ground allspice
1/4 tsp. ground cinnamon
1/8 tsp. ground nutmeg
2 tart apples, peeled, cored and diced
1 Tbsp. sugar

In a saucepan, combine shredded cabbage with all ingredients except apples and sugar. Cover and cook over moderate heat for 15 minutes, tossing several times so the cabbage will cook evenly.

Yield: .... 4 servings
Calories: 65
Fat: .... .350 g
Cholesterol: .... 0 mg
Dietary Exchanges:..... 1 Vegetable

Noreen Thomas, Nutritionist
Dakota Medical Center

TOMATO MEDLEY

1 tomato
1 cucumber
1 green pepper
1/2 cup reduced-calorie
    creamy Italian dressing

Slice tomato, cucumber, and green pepper into a salad bowl. Pour reduced-calorie creamy Italian dressing over the top.

Yield: .... 4 servings
Calories: 59
Fat: .... 3 g
Cholesterol: .... 2 mg
Sodium: .... 243 mg
Dietary Exchanges:..... 1 Vegetable
                            1/2 Fat

* Superfast Recipe

VEGETABLE ENCHILADAS

4 flour tortillas
1 cup shredded part-skim
   Monterey Jack cheese
1/2 cup part-skim Ricotta cheese
1/2 tsp. chili powder
1/4 tsp. cumin
1 cup tomato chunks
1/2 cup shredded zucchini
1/2 cup shredded carrots
1/3 cup chopped green pepper
1/4 cup chopped onion
1/2 cup chunky salsa sauce

Preheat oven to 350° F. (Recipe can be microwaved.) Combine tomato, zucchini, carrots, pepper, and onion in a 1-qt. baking dish and cover. Steam for 4 minutes in the MICROWAVE. Meanwhile, combine the cheese, chili powder, and cumin. Spread the cheese mixture over the tortillas. Spoon vegetable mixture on top. Roll up the tortillas and place seam side down in an 8-inch square baking dish sprayed with nonstick cooking spray. Pour the salsa over the top and bake for 25 minutes or MICROWAVE for 7 minutes on high power until bubbly.

Yield:	4 (1 tortilla each) servings
Calories:	251
Fat:	9 g
Cholesterol:	26 mg
Sodium:	348 mg
Dietary Exchanges:	2 Bread/Starch
	1 Lean Meat
	1 Fat
Preparation Time:	20 min. if microwaved

VEGETABLE ROLL-UPS

1/3 cup light pasteurized process cream
   cheese product (from 8-oz. container)
1/8 tsp. dried dill weed
1/8 tsp. garlic powder
4 (6 to 7-inch) flour tortillas
1/4 cup shredded carrots
1/4 cup chopped fresh broccoli
1 Tbsp. chopped green onions

In small bowl, combine cream cheese product, dill
and garlic powder; blend well. Spread about 1 Tbsp.
cream cheese mixture on each tortilla; top each with
carrot, broccoli and onions. Roll up each tortilla; cut
each in half.

Yield: .... 8 (one roll-up) servings
Calories: 70
Fat: .... 3 g
Cholesterol: .... 5 mg
Sodium: .... 120 mg
Dietary Exchanges:..... 1/2 Starch
                         1/2 Fat

WRAPPED CARROTS

4 med. carrots, cleaned and peeled
1/2 cup lite mayonnaise
2 Tbsp. dry buttermilk salad
    dressing mix
16 slices of thinly sliced lean
    turkey or dried beef
16 toothpicks

Cut the carrots into 4 pieces. Combine the mayonnaise and dressing mix. Dip each piece of carrot into the dressing and roll up in slices of dried beef or turkey. Secure with a toothpick.

Yield: .... 4 serving
Calories: 111
Fat: .... 8 g
Cholesterol: .... 21 mg
Sodium: .... 141 mg (using turkey)
Dietary Exchanges:..... 1 Vegetable
                         1 Lean Meat
                         1 Fat
Preparation Time: 15 min.

APPLE SALAD MOLD

1 pkg. (0.3 oz.) sugar-free cherry gelatin
1 cup boiling water
1/2 cup apple juice
1/2 cup cold water
1 med. unpeeled apple, chopped
   (about 1-1/2 cups)
1/2 cup chopped celery

Dissolve gelatin in boiling water. Combine juice and water. Add to gelatin and stir. Refrigerate until slightly thickened. Add apple and celery. Mix well. Refrigerate until set.

* Any flavor of gelatin may be substituted.

Yield:	2-1/2 cups
	5 (1/2 cup) servings
Calories:	35
Fat:	0 g
Cholesterol:	0 mg
Sodium:	52 mg
Carbohydrate:	7-1/2 g
Protein:	1 g
Dietary Exchanges:.....	1/2 fruit

ASPARAGUS CHEF SALAD

2-1/2 lb. asparagus, trimmed
8 oz. mushrooms, sliced
2 oz. part-skim julienne Swiss cheese
2 oz. lean julienne ham
1 Tbsp. finely chopped onion
1 orange, peeled and cubed

Dressing:
1 pkg. lemon and herb salad dressing mix
2 Tbsp. water
1/4 cup vinegar
1/4 cup vegetable oil

Chop asparagus into bite-sized pieces and place in a microwave-proof casserole dish. Add 2 Tbsp. water, cover, and MICROWAVE for 2 minutes. Drain. Measure remaining ingredients into a salad bowl. Add asparagus when completely cool. Prepare dressing in a shaker container and add approximately 1/3 of it to the salad. Save remaining dressing for greens and fresh vegetables.

Yield:	4 -1/2 (1 cup) servings
Calories:	151
Fat:	5 g
Cholesterol:	25 mg
Sodium:	347 mg
Dietary Exchanges:.....	2 Vegetable
	1 Lean Meat
	1 Fat
Preparation Time:	35 min.

CHICKEN AND FRUIT SALAD

Dressing:
1/3 cup nonfat strawberry yogurt
  (artificially sweetened)
1 Tbsp. reduced calorie mayonnaise
1 Tbsp. orange juice

2 cups cooked and cubed chicken or turkey
1 cup strawberries, halved
1 sm. banana, sliced
2 oranges, peeled and cut into chunks
1/2 cup sliced celery
1-1/2 cups seedless grapes
Lettuce leaves

Mix first three ingredients for dressing. Combine
remaining ingredients (except lettuce) and mix well
with dressing. Serve on lettuce leaves.

Yield: .... About 7-1/2 cups
                                  5 (1-1/2 cup) servings)
Calories: 200
Fat: .... 4 g
Cholesterol: .... 45 mg
Sodium: .... 82 mg
Dietary Exchanges:..... 1-1/2 Fruit
                                  2 Lean Meat

✸   ✸   ✸

CHICKEN AND SPINACH SALAD

6 oz. spinach, fresh
2 oranges, peeled and cut into chunks
2 cups cooked and cubed chicken
2 cups strawberries

Dressing:
3 Tbps. red wine vinegar
3 Tbsp. orange juice
1-1/2 Tbsp. oil (canola)
1/4 tsp. dry mustard
1/3 tsp. poppy seeds

Mix dressing ingredients and refrigerate. Wash spinach and tear into bite size pieces. Add oranges, chicken and strawberries. Serve with dressing.

Yield: .... 14 cups
7 servings (2 cup) servings
Calories: 135
Fat: .... 4 g
Cholesterol: .... 31 mg
Sodium: .... 46 mg
Dietary Exchanges:..... 1 Fruit
1-1/2 Lean Meat

CREAMY BROCCOLI CAULIFLOWER SALAD

1 bunch broccoli, cut into small florets
and stems chopped
1 head cauliflower, cut into small florets
1 red onion, chopped
1 to 1-1/2 tsp. garlic powder
1/2 to 1 tsp. salt
1 cup salad dressing or mayonnaise
1 cup sour cream

In large plastic food storage bag, combine broccoli,
cauliflower, onion, garlic powder and salt. Store in
refrigerator overnight.

Just before serving, drain vegetable mixture; place
in large bowl. In medium bowl, combine salad dressing and sour cream. Pour over vegetable mixture;
mix well. Store in refrigerator for up to 1 week.

Yield: .... 20 (1/2 cup) servings
Calories: 70
Fat: .... 5 g
Cholesterol: .... 7 mg
Sodium: .... 170 mg
Dietary Exchanges:..... 1 Vegetable
1 Fat

■ ■ ■ ■ ■

CRUNCHY COLESLAW

4 cups shredded cabbage
1 cup shredded carrots
1/3 cup chopped onion
6 oz. can frozen apple juice
    concentrate, thawed
1/4 cup cider vinegar
2 Tbsp. canola oil
1/2 tsp. celery seed
1/2 tsp. prepared mustard (low sodium)

In large bowl, toss cabbage, carrots and onions. In small bowl, combine remaining ingredients; pour over cabbage mixture. Toss well. Cover; refrigerate to blend flavors.

Yield: .... 8 (1/2 cup) servings
Calories: 55
Fat: .... 3.52 g
Cholesterol: .... 0 g
Sodium: .... 12 mg
Dietary Exchanges:..... 1 Vegetable
                                  1 Fat

Jan Sliper, LRD;
Robyn Vinje, MS, LRD;
Paula Anderson, LRD;
Kathy Tehven, LRD;
Lorraine Hanna, LRD
Dakota Medical Center

FILLING SPINACH SALAD

1 lb. freshly chopped spinach
4 oz. lean ham, diced
4 oz. Farmer's cheese, shredded
1/2 cup sliced scallions
1 10-oz. pkg. frozen peas, thawed

Dressing:
2 Tbsp. light mayonnaise
1/4 cup light sour cream
1/2 cup nonfat yogurt
2 tsp. Worcestershire sauce
1 tsp. lemon juice
1/2 tsp. white pepper

Combine spinach, ham, cheese, scallions and peas in a salad bowl. In a small bowl, whisk together ingredients for dressing. Pour dressing over salad just before serving.

NUTRITION ALERT: This recipe is high in sodium. It is intended for occasional use only. Substitute turkey for ham to reduce the sodium.

Yield: .... 4 (1 cup) servings
Calories: 228
Fat: .... 9 g
Cholesterol: .... 33 mg
Sodium: .... 636 mg
Dietary Exchanges:..... 3 Vegetables
                          2 Lean Meat
                          1 Fat
Preparation Time: .... 15 min.

GERMAN POTATO SALAD

4 lg. potatoes, boiled, peeled, and diced
3 strips bacon, diced, fried crisp,
   and drained well
4 green onions, diced

Dressing:
1/4 tsp. peppers
1 Tbsp. oil
4 Tbsp. vinegar
1 tsp. sugar
1/4 tsp. salt

Combine potatoes, bacon and onions in a bowl. Use a shaker jar to combine the dressing ingredients. Just before serving, pour dressing over the potatoes and toss. Serve at room temperature. Recipe is for 8 servings. It works well to use half the potato mixture and half the dressing for 2 meals of 4 servings each.

Yield:	8 (1/2 cup) servings
Calories:	94
Fat:	3 g
Cholesterol:	2 mg
Sodium:	92 mg
Dietary Exchanges:	1 Bread/Starch
	1/2 Fat
Preparation Time:	40 min.

HERB POTATO SALAD

The mustard and seasonings make this a tasty potato salad. Try using new red potatoes for added color.

> 1 lb. potatoes (about 4 cups)
> 1/2 cup sliced radishes (optional)
>
> *Dressing:*
> 3 Tbsp. nonfat plain yogurt
> 1 Tbsp. reduced calorie mayonnaise
> 1-1/2 tsp. Dijon mustard
> 1/2 tsp. garlic
> 1/2 tsp. dried basil
> 1/4 tsp. dried thyme
> 1/4 tsp. onion powder
> 1/4 tsp. salt (optional)

Scrub potatoes and cube. Place in medium saucepan and cover with water. Bring to a boil. Cover, reduce heat and simmer 12 minutes or until potatoes are done. Drain. Mix dressing ingredients. Combine hot potatoes, dressing and radishes. Serve hot or cold.

Yield:	6 servings
Calories:	80
Fat:	1 g
Cholesterol:	Trace
Sodium:	60 mg
Dietary Exchanges:	1 Starch

ITALIAN
CAULIFLOWER SALAD

3 cups fresh cauliflower, cut into flowerets
2 Tbsp. chopped green pepper
1-1/2 tsp. minced onion flakes
1/8 tsp. garlic powder
3 Tbsp. reduced-calorie Italian dressing
   (6 calories per Tbsp.)
1/8 tsp. dried basil
1/8 tsp. dried oregano
1/4 cup water
1/2 tsp. salt

Combine all ingredients in a medium saucepan.
Cook, covered, over medium heat until cauliflower
is tender, about 15 minutes. Chill. Serve cold.

Yield: .... 6 servings
Calories: 18
Fat: .... 1 g
Cholesterol: .... 0 mg
Sodium: .... 297 mg

LASAGNA SALAD

8 Pasta Growers lasagna noodles,
  cooked and drained
1 Tbsp. vegetable oil
1 cup low-fat cottage cheese
2 oz. shredded Mozzarella cheese
16 fresh spinach leaves, chopped
1/2 tsp. garlic powder
1 tsp. basil
1/4 tsp. black pepper
1 cup chopped tomatoes
1/2 cup low-calorie Italian dressing

Brush cooked noodles with oil. Combine cheeses, spinach, and garlic. Spread cheese mixture over noodles. Season with basil and pepper. Roll up noodles. Place on serving platter. Sprinkle with chopped tomatoes and your choice of low-calorie Italian dressing.

Yield: .... 4 (8 oz.) servings
Calories: .... 325 (per 2 noodle serving)
Fat: .... 10 g
Cholesterol: .... 17 mg
Sodium: .... 291 mg
Dietary Exchanges:..... 2 Bread/Starch
                          3 Lean Meat
Preparation Time: .... 20 minutes

LAYERED SUMMER SALAD

3 cups shredded lettuce or fresh
   greens of choice
1/2 cup low-calorie buttermilk dressing
2 strips of bacon, broiled and crumbled
2 cups cherry tomatoes, halved
2 oz. cubed part-skim Mozzarella cheese
8 oz. turkey or chicken, cooked and cubed

In a 3-quart salad bowl, layer the ingredients as
follows: lettuce, 1/4 cup dressing, bacon, tomatoes,
cheese, turkey or chicken, and remaining 1/4 cup
of dressing. Serve immediately or refrigerate overnight.

Yield: .... 4 (1-1/2 cup) servings
Calories: 208
Fat: .... 8 g
Cholesterol: .... 57 mg
Sodium: .... 637 mg
Dietary Exchanges:..... 1 Vegetable
                                      3 Lean Meat
Preparation Time: .... 20 minutes

Nutrition alert: This recipe is high in sodium. Reduce the sodium by omitting bacon, and by using
low-sodium cheese.

MARINATED PASTA SALAD

8 oz. Pasta Growers Rotini spirals
1/2 lb. fresh or frozen asparagus, cooked 5
   to 7 minutes and refreshed in ice water,
   cut into 1-inch pieces
1/2 cup julienne-cut red bell pepper
1/2 cup julienne-cut zucchini
1/2 cup finely chopped red onion
1/2 cup sliced celery
Several dashes crushed red pepper or hot
   pepper sauce
1/8 tsp. coarsely ground black pepper
1/4 tsp. bouquet garni
2 Tbsp. minced fresh parsley
1/4 cup reduced-calorie Italian dressing
3 Tbsp. white wine vinegar

Cook pasta according to package directions, omit
ting salt. Rinse, drain and cool. Place in a large bowl
Add vegetables and toss to mix. Add remaining in
gredients. Toss, cover and refrigerate several hours
or overnight. Serve on leaf lettuce with French bread
as an accompaniment.

Yield:	8 servings
Calories:	139
Fat:	1 gm
Cholesterol:	0 mg
Sodium:	135 mg
Dietary Exchanges:.....	1 Bread/Starch
	1 Vegetable

PEPPERONI PIZZA SALAD

6 oz. (2 cups) uncooked Pasta Growers rotini
3/4 cup refrigerated garden vegetable
    pasta sauce
1 Tbsp. olive oil
1/2 tsp. dried Italian seasoning
4 oz. (1 cup) shredded mozzarella cheese
1-3/4 oz. (1/3 cup) sm. pepperoni
    slices, halved
1 cup sliced fresh mushrooms
1 cup chopped green bell pepper
1/4 cup sliced black olives
1 tomato, chopped

Cook rotini to desired doneness as directed on package, omitting salt. Drain; rinse with cold water.

Meanwhile, in large bowl combine pasta sauce, oil and Italian seasoning; blend well. Add cooked rotini and remaining ingredients to pasta sauce mixture; toss gently to coat. Refrigerate until serving time.

Yield:	6 (1-1/4 cup) servings
Calories:	290
Fat:	11 g
Cholesterol:	17 mg
Sodium:	440 mg
Dietary Exchanges:	1 Vegetable
	1-1/2 Medium-Fat Meat

TEX MEX SLAW

1/2 head green cabbage
1 red onion, shredded
1 cup taco sauce
1/3 cup light mayonnaise
16 oz. can black beans, drained
12 oz. frozen whole kernel corn

Shred cabbage to desired texture. Transfer to a salad bowl. Shred onion and add to cabbage. Steam frozen corn for 3 minutes, then drain. Combine taco sauce and light mayonnaise. Toss cabbage, drained beans, and corn with taco sauce dressing just before serving.

Yield: .... 8 (1 cup) servings
Calories: 120
Fat: .... 3 g
Cholesterol: .... 3 mg
Sodium: .... 69 mg
Dietary Exchanges:..... 1/2 Bread/Starch
1 Vegetable
1 Fat
Preparation Time: .... 20 min.

WANT MORE SALAD

Kids love it!

    2 Granny Smith apples, cut fine
    3 stalks celery, chopped fine
    1/4 cup raisins
    2 Tbsp. sunflower seeds
    7 oz. pineapple chunks in juice, drained well

Dressing:
    1/4 cup light mayonnaise
    1/4 cup plain nonfat yogurt
    2 Tbsp. orange juice
    2 pkg. sugar substitute or 2 tsp. sugar

Combine first five ingredients in a salad bowl. Combine dressing ingredients and pour over fruits. Toss and refrigerate or serve. This keeps well for 2 days.

Yield: .... 4 (3/4 cup) servings
Calories: 155
Fat: .... 6 g
Cholesterol: .... 11 mg
Sodium: .... 155 mg
Dietary Exchanges:..... 1-1/2 Fruit
                               1 Fat
Preparation Time: .... 20 minutes

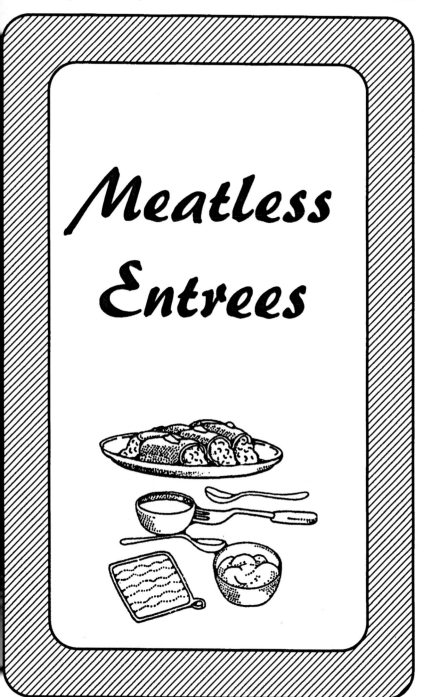

Meatless Entrees

WHAT'S BEHIND THE BEAN BOOM?

The high fiber diet can help with many health concerns including heart disease, diabetes, obesity, gastrointestinal disease, hypertension, and perhaps cancer.

Beans are also very economical.

HOW TO COOK LEGUMES

Dried beans, lentils, and split peas MUST BE COOKED before they are consumed. This helps modify toxins that can cause stomach cramps, nausea, and diarrhea.

Soaking Method: Soak in cold <u>water</u> for 6-8 hours or overnight at room temperature before cooking.

Quick Soak Method: 6-8 cups hot water is added for each pound of dry beans. The water is brought to a boil, and the legumes cooked for 2 minutes. Set aside, cover and let stand to soak 1 full hour. Drain and rinse and they're ready to cook.

In a slow cooker, legumes will take 10-12 hours at low heat, or 5-6 hours at high heat.

Legume Cooking Tips: Follow instructions regarding cooking times on the table provided.

Cook Tips: Use a very large kettle as legumes expand when cooked. Add a teaspoon of vegetable oil to prevent foaming. Don't add acidic products such as tomatoes, lemon juice, or vinegar when cooking - as this slows the softening process. Add only at the very end. Do not add baking soda.

Cooking Requirements:

1 cup dry = 1/2 lb. or 2-1/2 cups cooked beans

	Cooking Time (Hours)	Water (Cups)	Yield (Cups)
Black Beans	1-1/2	4	2
Garbanzo	3	4	4
Great Northern Beans	2	3-1/2	2
Kidney Beans	1-1/2	3	2
Pinto Beans	2-1/2	3	2
Soy Beans	3 or More	3	2

GARDEN SCRAMBLE

8 oz. carton egg substitute (1 cup)
1/8 tsp. black pepper
1/8 tsp. marjoram leaves
1/4 cup finely chopped celery
1/4 cup finely chopped red pepper
2 Tbsp. chopped green pepper
1 Tbsp. fat-free chicken broth
1 cup grated non-fat Cheddar cheese
2 slices white or whole wheat bread, toasted
    non-fat cooking spray
1 Tbsp. chopped chives

In a bowl, combine egg substitute, pepper, and marjoram; set aside. In a non-stick skillet sprayed with a non-fat cooking spray, over medium heat, cook celery, red pepper, green pepper, and chives in chicken broth until tender. Add Egg Beaters and grated cheese to mixture. Cook, stirring occasionally until set . Serve immediately over toast halves if desired or plain.

Yield: .... 2 servings
Calories: 181
Fat: .... 0 g
Cholesterol: .... 20 mg
Sodium: .... 774 mg
Dietary Exchanges:..... 1 Bread
                          1 Lean Meat

HOMEMADE EGG SUBSTITUTE

A whole egg contains 250 mg cholesterol while the egg substitute contains only 1 mg. The egg substitute will keep for a week in the refrigerator. Freezes well.

> 6 egg whites
> 1/4 cup non-fat dry milk powder
> 1 Tbsp. vegetable oil
> 6 drops yellow food coloring
>   (optional)

Combine all ingredients in a mixing bowl and blend until smooth. Refrigerate until used.

Yield: 3/4 cup; 1/4 cup equals 1 whole egg
Calories: 36
Fat: .... 1.5 g
Cholesterol: .... 1 mg
Sodium: .... 50 mg
Dietary Exchanges:..... 1/2 skim milk

KIDNEY BEAN TORTILLA

Stuff 8 6 -in. flour tortillas with a mixture of:

>   16 oz. (1 small can) drained kidney beans
>   1/2 cup chopped scallions
>   2 Tbsp. green chilies
>   4 oz. shredded part-skim cheese

Yield: .... 2 (6-inch) tortillas
Calories: 327
Fat: .... 7 g
Cholesterol: .... 15 mg
Sodium: .... 866 mg
Dietary Exchanges: ..... 2 Starch/Bread
                                  2 Vegetable
                                  2 Lean Meat

* Superfast Recipe

LOW-FAT REFRIED BEANS

1/2 cup chopped onion
1/2 cup fat-free chicken (broth)
2 cups canned pinto beans
   rinsed & drained (or fresh-cooked)
2 Tbsp. chili powder
2-3 tsp. ground cumin
1/2 tsp. lite salt (optional)
1/8 tsp. ground pepper
1/2 cup salsa (mild or spicy)

Heat fat free chicken broth in a 10-inch non-stick skillet over medium heat until hot. Add chopped onion and cook until soft. Add pinto beans; cook, stirring occasionally, 5 minutes. Mash beans; stir in chili powder, salsa, cumin, salt, and pepper. Add more liquid Butter Buds or chicken broth to skillet if necessary. Cook and stir until a smooth paste forms, about 5 minutes. Garnish with grated non-fat Cheddar cheese melted on top.

Yield: .... 6 servings
Calories: 86
Fat: .... 0.8 g
Cholesterol: .... 0 mg
Sodium: .... 533 mg
Dietary Exchanges:...... 1 Bread

MOCK DEVILED EGGS

1 (8 ounce) carton Egg Substitute
1 dozen eggs, boiled, peeled and
    sliced in half (discard yolks)
3 Tbsp. sweet pickle relish
1/4 cup fat-free Miracle Whip
    or mayonnaise
3 Tbsp. mustard
1/8 tsp. celery salt
Paprika for garnish

In an 8-inch non-stick skillet, pour in Egg Substitute. Cover tightly; cook over low heat 10 minutes or until just set. Remove from heat; let stand, covered for ten minutes. Remove from skillet and cool completely. Chop and place in a medium sized bowl. Add all the rest of the ingredients, except cooked egg whites, to the Egg mixture. Blend well with a fork. Using a small spoon, fill the egg whites with the Egg mixture. Sprinkle paprika on top of the Mock Deviled Eggs and refrigerate until ready to serve.

Yield: .... 24 mock deviled eggs
Calories: 19
Fat: .... 0.1 g
Cholesterol: .... 0 mg
Sodium: .... 115 mg
Dietary Exchanges:..... 1 Lean Meat

VEGETARIAN SUPPER DISH

1 cup uncooked regular rice
1 med. onion, chopped (1/2 cup)
2 garlic cloves, minced
2 Tbsp. oil (canola)
1 med. zucchini, coarsely chopped (1 cup)
1 med. green pepper, chopped (1 cup)
1/2 tsp. oregano leaves
1/8 tsp. pepper
2 med. tomatoes, peeled, coarsely chopped
16 oz. kidney beans, drained

Cook rice as directed on package, omitting salt. In large skillet, saute onion and garlic in oil until onion is tender. Add zucchini, green pepper, oregano and pepper; cook vegetables until tender-crisp, about 5 minutes. Add tomatoes and beans; cover and heat thoroughly. Spoon hot rice onto serving platter and spoon vegetable mixture over rice.

Yield: .... 7 (1 cup) servings
Calories: 218
Fat: .... 4.55 g
Cholesterol: .... 0 mg
Sodium: .... 127 mg
Dietary Exchanges:..... 2 Bread
                              1 Fat

Jan Sliper, RD; Robyn Vinje, MS, LRD
Paula Anderson, RD; Kathy Tehven, RD
Dakota Medical Center

Pasta, Potatoes & Rice

Dakota Growers Pasta Company
Retail Carton Availability (Including Prepared Dinners)

Product	Shape No.	8 oz.	12 oz.	16 oz.	32 oz.	48 oz.	Prepared Dinners	Tri-color
Angel Hair	01			■				
Vermicelli	02			■	■	■		
Thin Spaghetti	03	■		■	■	■		
Spaghetti	04	■		■	■	■		
Linguine	05			■	■	■		
Fettuccine	06		■	■				
Elbow Spaghetti	39	■						
Ditalini	08			■				
Elbow Macaroni	09	■		■	■	■	■ (7.25 oz.,14 oz.)	
Casserole Elbow	11			■				
Cut Macaroni	12			■			■ (7.25 oz.)	
Ziti	13			■				
Ziti Rigati	37			■				
Rigatoni	14			■				
Mini Rotini	32						■ (6.25 oz.,12 oz.)	
Rotini	20			■				■
Roletti	21			■				■
Fusilli	31			■				

One Pasta Ave. • P.O. Box 21 • Carrington, ND 58421-0021 USA • (701) 652-2855 • FAX (701) 652-3552

Dakota Growers Pasta Company
Retail Carton Availability (Including Prepared Dinners, cont.)

Product	Shape No.	8 oz.	12 oz.	16 oz.	32 oz.	48 oz.	Prepared Dinners	Tri-color
Small Shells	15	■		■			■ (7.25 oz.,12 oz.)	■
Medium Shells	16			■				■
Large Shells	17			■				
Jumbo Shells	41		■					
Penne	18			■				
Penne Rigate	19			■				
Nuggets	22			■				
Wagon Wheels	23			■				■
Orzo	25			■				
Alphabets	35			■				
Acini de Pepe	36			■				
Tubettini	40			■				
Rings	38	■						
Smooth Lasagna	07		■	■				
Ridged Lasagna	34		■	■				

PASTA FACTS

♥ • Pasta is an all-inclusive Italian word to describe all various shapes and sizes of products made of flour and water. Semolina is milled from the heart of durum wheat, the hardest and one of the purest of all wheats.

♥ • More than 150 pasta shapes are commercially available; some estimates indicate more than 350 shapes worldwide.

♥ • A five-ounce serving of cooked pasta contains 210 calories, 7 grams of protein, 41 grams of carbohydrates and 1 gram of fat. When cooked in unsalted water, pasta contains less than 0.5 milligrams of sodium per serving. Pasta contains six of the eight essential amino acids.

♥ • Americans eat more than 2 billion pounds of pasta annually – that's about 18.4 pounds per person in 1990.

♥ • If you measured the spaghetti from a very hearty meal, it would stretch nearly 150 feet laid end to end.

♥ • Seventy-five to eighty percent of durum wheat grown in the U.S. is produced in North Dakota.

♥ • Uncooked pasta can be stored for up to one year in the dark under normal conditions.

♥ • In America, Easterners buy more long goods (spaghetti, etc.); Midwesterners prefer short goods like macaroni. Specialty goods are usually popular in cities with a substantial Italian-American contingent.

Continued

PASTA FACTS (Continued)

♥ • Pasta can cut a family's meat budget by 30-50 percent. Pasta can extend an entree having only a pound of meat to a meal large enough to satisfy six hungry adults.

♥ • Versatile pasta can be served as a tempting main dish every night for a year without once repeating a recipe.

♥ • Pasta is an excellent source of complex carbohydrates. Simple carbohydrates, like sugar, give a quick lift that disappears within minutes . . . but their calories can stay behind to plague weight conscious dieters. Complex carbohydrates must be broken down for digestion, and supply the brain and muscles with a slower, constant source of energy. They also satisfy hunger longer, yet without a heavy price to pay in added calories.

LONG GOODS	SHORT GOODS	SPECIALTY GOODS
Spaghetti	Macaroni	Rigatoni
Vermicelli	Shells	Rotini Twists Twirls
Linguine		Mostaccioli
Fettuccine		Ziti

Source:
National Pasta Association

From Our Family to Yours -

Ziti

Elbow Spaghetti

Rotini

Linguine

Penne Rigate

Elbow Macaroni

Dakota Growers Pasta Company is the world's first grower-owned pasta cooperative. The seed of an idea was planted by a group of North Dakota farmers in 1991 when a feasibility study was conducted. Tim Dodd, General Manager, and Gary Mackintosh, National Sales Manager were hired to oversee plant operations and marketing efforts. On January 6, 1992, the management team joined the interim board of directors to sign up farmers from across North Dakota to invest in the pasta manufacturing venture.

The co-op signed up 1,042 farmers who invested $12 million to build the $40 million durum mill and pasta plant. Ground breaking ceremonies took place in Carrington on July 9, 1992 and construction began on September 9. Fast track construction had the plant producing its first pounds of elbow macaroni just 14 months later, less than two years after the first grower information meeting!

Dakota Growers is very proud of its pasta. We feel it is simply the best pasta available and hope you and your family will enjoy this healthy product.

Thank you for your interest and support in Pasta Growers pasta.

Dakota Growers Pasta Company

ASPARAGUS FETTUCCINE

8 oz. dry Pasta Growers fettuccine, cooked
   and tossed with
1 lb. steamed asparagus cuts
4 oz. Parmesan cheese

Yield: .... 4 servings
Calories: 368
Fat: .... 8 g
Cholesterol: .... 19 mg
Sodium: .... 457 mg
Dietary Exchanges:.... 2-1/2 Starch/Bread
                         2 Vegetable
                         2 Lean Meat

*SUPERFAST RECIPE

CRAB SPAGHETTI

8 oz. dry Pasta Growers spaghetti,
  cooked and tossed with
8 oz. mock crab, flaked
5 oz. (or one-half of a small can) low fat,
  low sodium cream of mushroom soup
2 tsp. dried cilantro
  and/or 1 Tbsp. green chilies

Yield:	4 servings
Calories:	322
Fat:	4 g
Cholesterol:	12 mg
Sodium:	652 mg
Dietary Exchanges:....	3 Starch/Bread
	1 Vegetable
	1 Lean Meat

*SUPERFAST RECIPE

CURRIED TURKEY MANICOTTI

SAUCE:
1/2 cup finely chopped onion
1/2 cup finely chopped
  green bell pepper
1/4 cup finely chopped celery
1 Tbsp. canola or vegetable oil
2 Tbsp. all-purpose flour
1 Tbsp. curry powder
3/4 tsp. ground cumin
2 cups low-sodium
  chicken broth
2 cups seeded chopped
  plum tomatoes
2 Tbsp. dark raisins

FILLING:
7 oz. ground turkey
  or chicken
1/2 cup finely shredded
  zucchini
1/2 cup finely shredded
  fresh spinach
1 egg
1/2 tsp. salt
1/8 tsp. freshly ground
  black pepper
4-1/2 oz. Pasta Growers
  manicotti shells, cooked
  and drained (about 6)

Reserve 1 Tbsp. each onion, bell pepper and celery; set aside for filling. To prepare sauce, in large nonstick skillet, heat oil; add remaining onion, bell pepper and celery. Cook over medium-high heat stirring frequently, until onion is translucent, about 3 minutes.

Add flour, curry and cumin to vegetables; toss lightly to coat. Cook 1 minute. Stir in chicken broth; bring to a boil. Reduce heat to medium; cook, stirring, until mixture thickens slightly. Add tomatoes and raisins; stir to combine. Reduce heat to low; simmer, covered, stirring frequently, 10 minutes.

Preheat oven to 350° F. Spray an 11/17" baking pan with nonstick cooking spray.

In medium bowl, combine reserved vegetables and all filling ingredients, mixing thoroughly. Spoon about 3 Tbsp. filling into each manicotti shell. Arrange filled shells in pan; top with sauce. Cover with foil; bake 25 minutes, or until filling is set and sauce is bubbly.

Yield:	3 servings
Calories:	434
Fat:	15 g
Cholesterol:	119 mg
Sodium:	518 mg
Dietary Exchanges:	2 Breads, 3 Vegetables, 2 Meats, 1 Fat

Susan Fuglie - Dakota Medical Center

FETTUCCINE ALFREDO WITH VEGETABLES

6 oz. uncooked Pasta Growers fettuccine
2 tsp. margarine
1/4 cup flour
1 cup chicken broth
1 cup milk
1/2 tsp. dried basil leaves
1/3 cup grated Parmesan cheese
1 (14 oz.) pkg. frozen broccoli and
    red peppers, thawed, drained
Coarsely ground black pepper

Cook fettuccine to desired doneness as directed on package. Meanwhile, melt margarine in medium saucepan. Stir in flour until blended. Gradually stir in broth, milk and basil; cook until slightly thickened, stirring constantly. Stir in Parmesan cheese; blend well.

Drain fettuccine; return to pan. Add sauce and vegetables; toss to coat. Sprinkle with pepper. Cook over low heat until thoroughly heated. If desired, serve with additional Parmesan cheese.

Yield: .... 5 (1 cup) servings
Calories: 240
Fat: .... 6 g
Cholesterol: .... 41 mg
Sodium: .... 350 mg
Dietary Exchanges:.... 2 Starch
                         1 Vegetable
                         1 Fat

FETTUCCINE LOW-FAT ALFREDO

8 oz. Pasta Growers fettuccine, cooked tender
4 cups vegetables cut into bite-sized pieces
  (such as broccoli, carrots, red pepper, pea pods,
  zucchini, mushrooms, and onions)
1 tsp. margarine
1/4 tsp. garlic powder
1 cup part-skim Ricotta cheese
2 Tbsp. Parmesan cheese
2 Tbsp. skim milk
1 egg or 1/4 cup liquid egg substitute
1/4 tsp. salt (optional)
1/2 tsp. oregano
1/8 tsp. pepper

Cook fettuccine according to package directions. Meanwhile
microwave vegetables in a covered dish with 1 Tbsp. water
for 3 minutes. At the same time, melt margarine in a sauce
pan and add garlic powder. Stir to mix. Blend in cheeses,
skim milk, egg, and seasonings. Bring to a boil, reduce heat
to low, and cook for 3 minutes. Transfer this sauce to a
blender and blend smooth. Drain noodles and vegetables
well. Transfer to serving bowl. Pour sauce over noodles and
vegetables and toss gently. Serve.

Yield:	8 (1 cup) servings
Calories:	200
Fat:	6 g
Cholesterol:	43 mg with egg
	11 mg with substitute
Sodium:	137 mg with salt
	75 mg without salt
Dietary Exchanges:.....	1 Bread/Starch, 1 Skim Milk,
	1 Fat
Preparation Time:	30 minutes

MACARONI AND BEAN BAKE

1 (7 oz.) pkg. Pasta Growers macaroni, cooked and drained
2 cups non-fat Cheddar cheese, grated
1 (16 oz.) can pinto, ranch, or red beans (your choice), undrained
1 (16 oz.) can stewed tomatoes (Italian or Mexican style)
1 green pepper, diced
1 red pepper, diced
2 Tbsp. fat-free Parmesan cheese

Heat oven to 375° F. Spray a 9-inch square glass baking dish with a non-fat cooking spray. Combine macaroni, 1-1/2 cups Cheddar cheese, beans, tomatoes, and peppers; mix well. Spoon into prepared dish. Sprinkle with remaining Cheddar cheese and Parmesan cheese. Bake 25 to 30 minutes or until heated through. Let stand 10 minutes before serving.

Yield: .... 9 servings
Calories: 155
Fat: .... 0.7 g
Cholesterol: .... 0 mg
Sodium: .... 434 mg
Dietary Exchanges:.... 1 Bread
                          1 Milk

MEXICAN STUFFED SHELLS

Pasta shells hold all the taco-like ingredients in this dish, which yo
can eat with your hands or a knife and fork.

> 13 oz. lean ground beef, broiled 2 minutes
> 1/2 cup chopped onion
> 1 garlic clove, minced
> 1 tsp. chili powder
> 1/4 tsp. ground cumin
> 1/4 tsp. dried oregano
> 1/4 tsp. salt
> 1/2 cup spicy or mild salsa
> 1/4 cup light sour cream
> 3 oz. jumbo Pasta Growers pasta shells,
>   cooked and drained (about 12)
> 1-1/2 oz. coarsely shredded reduced-fat sharp
>   Cheddar cheese
> 1/2 cup shredded lettuce
> 2 Tbsp. diced seeded tomato

Preheat oven to 350° F. Spray an 11/7" baking pan with nonstic
cooking spray.

In large nonstick skillet, combine beef, onion and garlic. Cook
over medium high heat, stirring frequently to break up beef, unti
beef is browned and onion is translucent, about 5 minutes.

Add chili powder, cumin, oregano and salt; toss to mix well. Coo
1 minute. Stir in salsa; cook, stirring frequently, 5 minutes. Remov
from heat; stir in sour cream. Let cool slightly.

Stuff shells evenly with meat mixture, mounding slightly. Arrang
shells in baking pan; cover with foil. Bake 15 minutes; uncover an
sprinkle evenly with cheese. Bake, uncovered, just until cheese melts
1-2 minutes. Top shells evenly with lettuce and tomato.

Yield:	4 servings
Calories:	406
Fat:	24 g
Cholesterol:	82 mg
Sodium:	463 mg
Dietary Exchanges:	1 Bread, 3/4 Vegetable, 3 Meat

MOZZARELLA MACARONI

8 oz. dry Pasta Growers macaroni,
  cooked and tossed with
8 oz. no added salt tomato sauce
2 tsp. dried basil
8 oz. shredded part-skim mozzarella cheese

For perfect pasta, bring 2 quarts of water in a one-gallon pot to a boil. Do not use a small pan because it will boil over and you'll be cleaning up a messy stove. Add 8 ounces of pasta and boil rapidly (keep the bubbles coming to ensure tender noodles). Boil for 8 to 12 minutes or follow package directions. Set the time so it doesn't overcook. Drain noodles in a colander and rinse with cold water, toss as you rinse.

Yield: .... 4 servings
Calories: 337
Fat: .... 6 g
Cholesterol: .... 15 mg
Sodium: .... 163 mg
Dietary Exchanges:.... 3 Starch/Bread
                         2 Vegetables
                         1 Lean Meat

* Superfast Recipe

ONE DISH LASAGNA

32 oz. low-sodium spaghetti sauce
12 oz. raw Pasta Growers lasagna noodles
1 lb. lean ground beef, browned
1/4 cup onion, chopped
8 oz. lowfat cottage cheese (1% fat)
8 (1 oz.) slices American cheese (1% fat)
8 oz. mozzarella cheese (skim)
1 Tbsp. Parmesan cheese
1-1/2 cups hot water

Layer a 9x13 inch pan as follows:
Cover bottom with 1/3 sauce, layer raw noodles, hal
of meat in small chunks, onions, cottage cheese, 1/
3 of sauce, layer raw noodles, American cheese slices
rest of meat, rest of sauce. Layer mozzarella cheese
on top. Press down. Add hot water. Press down
Sprinkle Parmesan cheese on top. Cover with foi
and bake at 375° for 1 hour. Remove foil; bake 45
minutes longer (or less) until thick or set up. Noodles
and meat will be done.

Yield:	16 servings
Calories:	270
Fat:	12.72 g
Cholesterol:	56.42 mg
Sodium:	294 mg
Dietary Exchanges:....	1 Bread/Starch
	1 Vegetable
	2 Lean Meat
	2 Fat

SPICY TUNA PASTA TOSS

6 oz. tri-colored Pasta Growers corkscrew pasta
2 cans white tuna in spring water, drained
1/2 cup yellow pepper strips
1/2 cup quartered cherry tomatoes
1/4 cup diced celery
3/4 cup salsa
1/2 cup reduced-calorie mayonnaise
1/2 tsp. red pepper
2 Tbsp. sliced green onions

Cook pasta according to package directions; rinse under cold water and drain. Combine pasta, tuna and next three ingredients. Combine salsa, mayonnaise and red pepper. Add to pasta mixture; toss. Cover and chill. Sprinkle with green onions.

Yield:	6 servings
Calories:	171
Fat:	5.22 g
Cholesterol:	37.3 mg
Sodium:	337 mg
Dietary Exchanges:	1 Bread
	2 Lean Meat
	1 Fat

Christy Arnold, RD
Dakota Medical Center

TEX-MEX
MACARONI AND CHEESE

1 (7-1/4 oz.) pkg. macaroni and cheese dinner
1/3 cup skim milk
1 Tbsp. margarine (sunflower or corn oil)
1 cup frozen whole kernel corn
1/4 tsp. chili powder
1 (8 oz.) can kidney beans, drained
1 (4 oz.) can diced green chilies, drained
1 med. tomato, chopped

Cook macaroni in boiling water as directed on package; drain. Add milk, margarine and cheese sauce packet; mix well. Stir in remaining ingredients. Cook until thoroughly heated, stirring occasionally.

Yield: .... 4 (1-1/4 cup) servings
Calories: 320
Fat: .... 6 g
Cholesterol: .... 7 mg
Sodium: .... 520 mg
Dietary Exchanges:.... 3-1/2 Starch
1/2 High-Fat Meat

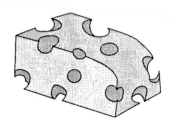

TUNA STUFFED MANICOTTI

8 cooked Pasta Growers manicotti shells
2 (5 oz.) cans water packed tuna, drained
1/2 cup nonfat cottage cheese
1 Tbsp. dried parsley
1/4 cup diced onions
1 tsp. lemon juice
1/4 tsp. dill weed
SAUCE:
1/2 cup nonfat cottage cheese, blended smooth
1/2 cup plain nonfat yogurt
1/4 tsp. dill weed
1/8 tsp. garlic powder
TOPPING:
2 Tbsp. Parmesan cheese

Cook manicotti according to package directions. Drain and cool. Combine tuna, cottage cheese, parsley, onions, lemon juice, and dill weed in a small mixing bowl. Stuff manicotti shells with tuna mixture and place seam side down in a 7 x 11-inch baking dish sprayed with non-stick cooking spray. Combine ingredients for the sauce and spoon over manicotti. Sprinkle with Parmesan cheese. Bake 350° F. for 30 minutes or microwave for 8 minutes on high power.

Yield:	4 (2 shells) servings
Calories:	285
Fat:	3 g
Cholesterol:	76 mg
Sodium:	327 mg
Dietary Exchanges:	1 Bread/Starch
	2 Lean Meat
	1 Skim Milk
Preparation Time:	25 minutes, if microwaved

BAKED POTATO BURRITO

4 potatoes
1 Tbsp. vegetable oil
1 cup chopped onions
1/2 tsp. garlic powder
2 tsp. chili powder
2 tsp. cumin
1/2 tsp. oregano
1/2 tsp. pepper
1/4 tsp. salt
1 lb. lean hamburger
1 Tbsp. tomato paste
1/2 cup bottled salsa
3 cups shredded lettuce
3 tomatoes, cubed
1 oz. part-skim Cheddar cheese, shredded

Bake potatoes in MICROWAVE (8 to 12 minutes on high power, turning once during cooking.) Cool, then slice in half lengthwise. Scoop out half the pulp from each piece and set aside. Meanwhile, heat oil over medium heat in a large skillet. Add onions and saute 5 minutes. Add spices and cook 1 minute. Add ground beef and cook until browned. Pour mixture into a colander and drain off all fat, pressing meat to promote draining. Stir in reserved potato pulp, tomato paste, and salsa. Stuff the potato shells with prepared meat filling. Place on a baking sheet, and cover with cheese. Broil 6 to 8 minutes until cheese is melted. Serve with lettuce and tomatoes on the side.

Yield:	8 servings
Calories:	232
Fat:	6 g
Cholesterol:	36 mg
Sodium:	238 mg
Dietary Exchanges:	1 Bread/Starch
	3 Vegetable
	1-1/2 Lean Meat
Preparation Time:	45 min.

FLUFFY SWEET POTATO SOUFFLE'

3 cups mashed, peeled, cooked sweet
   potatoes (about 2 large)
1/4 cup brown sugar
   (or 2 Tbsp. brown sugar and 1/2 tsp.)
4 egg whites or 1 cup egg substitute
1/4 cup light rum (or 1 tsp. rum extract)
1/2 - 1 tsp. cinnamon

Preheat oven to 350°. Combine mashed sweet potatoes with the rest of the ingredients. Beat well with
a hand mixer. Fold into a 2-quart baking dish that
has been sprayed with a non-fat cooking spray. Bake
for 45-50 minutes or until a knife inserted into the
center comes out clean and top is firm and golden
brown.

Yield: .... 6-8 servings
Calories: .... 204 (All Sugar)
                               193 (1/2 Sweet 'N Low)
Fat: .... 4 g
Cholesterol: .... 0 mg
Sodium: .... 63 mg
Dietary Exchanges:..... 2 Breads
                               1/2 Fruit

LOW FAT FRENCH FRIES

This is a children's favorite that is so easy to prepare!

> 4 med. potatoes (5 oz. each)
> 1 Tbsp. oil (canola or olive)
> Salt to taste (optional)
> Malt vinegar to taste

Preheat oven to 475°. Scrub potatoes but don't peel Cut into half inch slices or strips. Place potato slices in a plastic bag with the oil and shake well to coa potatoes evenly. Spray baking sheet with a non-stick cooking spray. Arrange potatoes in a single layer and bake for 30 minutes, or until golden brown, turning potatoes every 10 minutes. Sprinkle with salt (op tional), and serve with malt vinegar.

Yield:	4 servings
Calories:	185
Fat:	4 g
Cholesterol:	0 mg
Sodium:	11 mg
Dietary Exchanges:.....	2 Starch
	1/2 Fat

Variation: Temperature may be decreased to 450° and baking time increased to 40 minutes.

OVEN FRIES

3 med. unpeeled baking potatoes
(about 1-1/2 lbs.)
2 lg. carrots, peeled
2 tsp. vegetable oil
1/4 tsp. salt
1/8 tsp. pepper

Scrub potatoes; cut potatoes and carrots into 3-1/2" x 1/2" x 1/2" strips. Pat dry with paper towels. Combine oil, salt and pepper in a large bowl. Add potatoes and carrots and toss to coat. Arrange in a single layer on a baking sheet coated with non-fat cooking spray. Bake at 475° for 25 minutes until tender and brown, turning after 15 minutes.

Yield: .... 6 (1/2 cup) servings
Calories: 141
Fat: .... 1.79 g
Cholesterol: .... 0 mg
Sodium: .... 247 mg
Dietary Exchanges:..... 1 Bread

Christy Arnold, LRD
Dakota Medical Center

PARMESAN POTATOES

4 med. potatoes, scrubbed
2 Tbsp. flour
2 Tbsp. Parmesan cheese
Pepper to taste
2 Tbsp. margarine
1/2 tsp. paprika

Melt margarine in 9x13 pan. Cut each potato into 4
to 6 chunks with skins on. In a plastic bag, combine
flour, Parmesan and pepper. Shake potatoes, a few
at a time, in cheese mixture. Place potatoes in a single
layer and bake turning once during baking. Bake at
350° for 60 minutes.

Yield: .... 4 servings
Calories: 71
Fat: .... 3.62 g
Cholesterol: .... 1.96 mg
Sodium: .... 186 mg
Dietary Exchanges: ..... 1 Bread

TWICE BAKED POTATOES

4 med. potatoes, baked
1 cup low-fat cottage cheese
1/2 cup low-fat milk
1 Tbsp. onion, minced
   freshly ground black pepper
   paprika
   dried parsley flakes

Cut hot potatoes in half lengthwise. Scoop out potatoes, leaving skins intact for restuffing. With wire whisk, beat potatoes with cottage cheese, milk and onion. Spoon mixture back into skins. Sprinkle with paprika flakes and black pepper. Bake 10 minutes until just golden.

Calories: 72.7
Fat: .... 7 g
Cholesterol: .... 3 mg
Sodium: .... 316 mg
Cito: .... 7.78 mg
Rro: .... 8.53 g
Dietary Exchanges:..... 1 Bread

Noreen Thomas, Nutritionist
Dakota Medical Center

WONDERFUL STUFFED POTATOES

4 med. baking potatoes
3/4 cup (1%) or non-fat cottage cheese
1/4 cup nonfat (1% or skim) milk
2 Tbsp. margarine
1 tsp. dill weed
3/4 tsp. herb seasoning
4-6 drops hot pepper sauce
2 tsp. grated parmesan cheese

Prick potatoes with fork. Bake at 425° for 60 minutes or until fork is easily inserted. Cut potatoes in half lengthwise. Carefully scoop out potato leaving about 1/2" of pulp inside shell. Mash pulp in large bowl. Mix in by hand remaining ingredients except parmesan cheese. Spoon mixture into potato shells. Sprinkle each half with 1/4 tsp. parmesan cheese. Place on baking sheet and return to oven. Bake 15-20 minutes or until tops are golden brown.

Yield: .... 4 servings
Calories: 90
Fat: .... 3.5 g
Cholesterol: .... 3 mg
Sodium: .... 343 mg
Dietary Exchanges:..... 1 Bread/Starch
                         1 Lean Meat

✳   ✳   ✳   ✳

BROCCOLI RICE CASSEROLE

1/2 cup diced celery
1/2 cup chopped onion
1/2 lb. fresh mushrooms
2 Tbsp. margarine
2 10 oz. pkgs. chopped broccoli
1 cup quick rice, uncooked
2 oz. Light American cheese, shredded
2/3 cup Cream Soup Substitute or reduced
    fat, reduced sodium cream soup

Preheat oven to 350° F. (Recipe can also be microwaved.) In a no-stick skillet, saute onion, celery, and sliced mushrooms in margarine until tender. Using 1 large or two small casserole dishes, combine sauteed vegetables with broccoli, rice, and shredded cheese. Combine 2/3 cup Cream Soup Substitute with 2-1/2 cups water in a shaker container. Add to the other ingredients and mix well. Bake for 30 minutes or MICROWAVE on high power for 15 to 18 minutes, until mixture is bubbly.

Yield: .... 4 1-1/2 cup servings
Calories: .... 132 per serving
Fat: .... 5 g
Cholesterol: .... 4 mg
Sodium: .... 302 mg
Dietary Exchange: ...... 1 Bread/Starch
                          1 Vegetable
                          1 Fat
Preparation Time: .... 45 min.

HAWAIIAN RICE MEDLEY

1 cup pineapple juice or water
1/2 to 1 cup frozen mixed vegetables
1/4 cup chopped green onions
2 tsp. margarine
1 tsp. lite soy sauce
1/4 tsp. very low-sodium chicken-flavor
   instant bouillon
1 cup uncooked instant rice

In medium saucepan, combine pineapple juice, vegetables, onions, margarine, soy sauce and bouillon
Bring to a boil. Reduce heat to medium; cook unti
vegetables are of desired doneness. Stir in rice; remove from heat. Cover; let stand 5 to 7 minutes or
until liquid is absorbed.

Yield: .... 4 servings
Calories: 170
Fat: .... 2 g
Cholesterol: .... 0 mg
Sodium: .... 100 mg
Dietary Exchanges:..... 1-1/2 Starch
                         1 Vegetable
                         1/2 Fat

RICE LASAGNA

1 (14 oz.) jar spaghetti sauce
1 (2.5 oz.) jar sliced mushrooms, drained
1 cup lowfat ricotta or cottage cheese
4 oz. (1 cup) shredded Mozzarella cheese
1 egg white
3 cups cooked rice
2 Tbsp. freshly grated Parmesan cheese

MICROWAVE DIRECTIONS: Spray 8-inch-square (1-1/2-quart) microwave-safe dish with nonstick cooking spray. In small bowl, combine spaghetti sauce and mushrooms; set aside. In another small bowl, combine ricotta cheese, Mozzarella cheese and egg white; mix well. In spray-coated dish, layer one-third of sauce, half of rice and half of ricotta cheese mixture; repeat layers. Spread remaining sauce on top.

Microwave on HIGH for 5 minutes; rotate dish 1/2 turn. Microwave on MEDIUM for 10 to 15 minutes or until thoroughly heated in center. Sprinkle with Parmesan cheese.

Yield: .... 6 servings
Calories: 330
Fat: .... 11 g
Cholesterol: .... 24 mg
Sodium: .... 580 mg
Dietary Exchanges:..... 2 Starch
2 Vegetable
1 1/2 Medium-Fat Meat

SOUTHWESTERN RICE

1-1/4 cups chicken broth
1 teaspoon cumin
1 to 2 teaspoons chili powder
1/4 tsp. hot pepper sauce,
    if desired
1 cup uncooked instant brown rice
1-1/2 cups frozen corn with red and
  green peppers
1/3 cup sliced green onions
1 Tbsp. chopped fresh cilantro

In medium saucepan, bring broth, cumin, chili powder and hot pepper sauce to a boil; stir in rice. Reduce heat; cover and simmer 5 to 10 minutes or
until rice is tender and liquid is absorbed. Stir in
corn with peppers, onions and cilantro; cook until
thoroughly heated.

Yield: .... 6 (1/2 cup) servings
Calories: 90
Fat: .... 1 g
Cholesterol: .... 0 mg
Sodium: .... 180 mg
Dietary Exchanges:..... 1 Starch

TACO RICE

1-1/4 cups water
1 (1-1/4 oz.) pkg. taco seasoning mix
1/2 cup chopped green bell pepper
1/2 cup chopped onion
1 cup frozen corn
1 (16-oz.) can stewed tomatoes, undrained
1 (8-oz.) can kidney beans, drained
1-1/2 cups uncooked instant brown rice
2 oz. (1/2 cup) shredded reduced-fat
   Cheddar cheese

In large skillet, combine all ingredients except rice and cheese. Bring to a boil; stir in rice. Reduce heat to low; cover and simmer 8 to 10 minutes or until liquid is absorbed, stirring occasionally. Remove from heat. Fluff mixture with fork; sprinkle with cheese. Cover; let stand 1 to 2 minutes or until cheese is melted.

Yield: .... 5 (1/2 cup) servings
Calories: 260
Fat: .... 4 g
Cholesterol: .... 8 mg
Sodium: .... 910 mg
Dietary Exchanges:..... 2 Starch
                          1 Vegetable
                          1 Lean Meat

VEGETARIAN FRIED RICE

1/2 cup sliced fresh mushrooms
1/2 cup shredded carrot
1/4 cup sliced green onions
1/4 cup chopped green bell pepper
1/4 tsp. ginger
1 garlic clove, minced
3 cups cooked brown rice
2 Tbsp. lite soy sauce
2 eggs, beaten
1/8 tsp. pepper
3/4 cup frozen sweet peas, thawed

Spray large nonstick skillet with nonstick cooking spray. Heat over medium heat until hot. Add mushrooms, carrot, green onions, bell pepper, ginger and garlic. Cook and stir 1 minute. Stir in rice and soy sauce. Cook over low heat for 5 minutes, stirring occasionally with fork.

Push rice mixture to side of skillet; add eggs and pepper to the other side. Cook over low heat for 4 minutes, stirring constantly until eggs are cooked. Add peas to rice and egg mixture; stir gently to combine. Cook until thoroughly heated. Serve with additional soy sauce, if desired.

Yield:	4 (1 cup) servings
Calories:	240
Fat:	4 g
Cholesterol:	106 gm
Sodium:	390 mg
Dietary Exchanges:.....	2 Starch
	1 Vegetable
	1/2 Lean Meat
	1/2 Fat

Poultry

&

Fish

BAKED CHIMICHANGAS

8 (6 inch) flour tortillas

Filling:
1-1/2 cups cooked and cubed chicken
2 oz. grated, low fat cheese
3/4 cup salsa, thick and chunky
Optional: Extra salsa
            Non-fat sour cream

Preheat oven to 400° F. Mix filling ingredients. Warm tortillas until pliable (about 5 seconds each in microwave or in a non-stick skillet). Wet one side of tortilla and place wet side down. Spoon on filling ingredients. Fold to hold in filling. Spray baking dish with non-stick coating. Lay chimichangas, seam side down, on baking dish. Bake for 15 minutes.

Yield:	4 (2 chimichangas) servings
Calories:	275
Fat:	6 g
Cholesterol:	46 mg
Sodium:	445 mg
Dietary Exchanges:....	2 Starch
	2 Lean Meat

Variations: Divide filling onto four large tortillas. Substitute ground or diced beef, pork, or turkey for chicken.

Sodium is figured for bottled salsa.

CHICKEN AND CHILI TORTILLA

8 (6 inch) flour tortillas
8 oz. cooked chicken pieces
5 oz. reduced fat, reduced salt cream of
    chicken soup
2 Tbsp. green chilis

Combine chicken pieces, soup and chilis. Stuff tortillas.

Yield:	4 (2 tortilla) servings
Calories:	257
Fat:	6 g
Cholesterol:	41 mg
Sodium:	497 mg
Dietary Exchanges:....	2 Starch/Bread
	2 Lean Meat

SUPERFAST RECIPE

CHICKEN CACCIATORE ONE

1 cup sliced mushrooms
1 cup tomato sauce
1 No. 2 can Italian tomatoes (16 oz.)
1/2 cup white wine (or cooking wine)
1/4 tsp. basil
1/4 tsp. oregano
1 bay leaf
1/2 tsp. lite salt (optional)
2 tsp. minced garlic (in a jar)
1 chopped onion
4 half chicken breasts, skinned and
    boned (chopped)
2 Tbsp. fat-free chicken broth

Heat liquid chicken broth in a non-stick skillet and brown chicken, onion, and garlic. Add all other ingredients except mushrooms. Bring to a boil, then cover and simmer about 30 minutes. Add mushrooms, cook 10 minutes more. Remove chicken from pan, boil down sauce until slightly thickened. Serve over cooked pasta.

Yield: .... 6 servings
Calories: 217
Fat: .... 3.5 g
Cholesterol: .... 73 mg
Sodium: .... 676 mg
Dietary Exchanges:.... 1 Bread
                         4 Lean Meat

CHICKEN CACCIATORE CAPELLINI

6 oz. Pasta Growers angel hair pasta, uncooked
4 (4 oz.) skinned, boned chicken breast halves
1-1/4 cups coarsely chopped onion
1-1/4 cups coarsely chopped green
    bell pepper
2 cups commercial low-fat, low-sodium
    spaghetti sauce
1/4 tsp. salt

Cook pasta according to package directions, omit
ting salt and fat. Drain pasta, and set aside.

Place a nonstick skillet over medium-high hea
until hot. Add chicken, onion, and bell pepper. Cool
chicken 3 minutes on each side or until lightly
browned, stirring vegetables occasionally.

Add spaghetti sauce and salt. Cover, reduce heat
and simmer 15 minutes or until chicken is done
Serve chicken mixture over pasta.

Yield: .... 4 (1 breast half,
                                   1 cup pasta, 3/4 cup
                                   sauce) servings
Calories: 365
Fat: .... 3 g
Cholesterol: .... 71 mg
Sodium: .... 596 mg
Dietary Exchanges:.... 1 Starch
                                   1 Vegetable
                                   1 Lean Meat

CHICKEN FAJITAS

1 lb. boneless, skinless chicken breasts,
   cut into 1-inch strips
3 Tbsp. lime juice
1/2 tsp. coriander
1/2 tsp. chili powder
1 green pepper, sliced
1 onion, sliced
8 (6 inch) flour tortillas
Salsa (Optional)

Mix lime juice with coriander and chili powder and pour over chicken. Set aside. Meanwhile, slice vegetables. Add to chicken and mix well. Spray pan with non-stick coating and stir-fry chicken and vegetables until done. Warm tortillas in microwave about 50 seconds on high or in non-stick skillet. Fill each tortilla with chicken mixture and serve with salsa.

Yield: .... 4 (2 filled tortillas) servings
Calories: 320
Fat: .... 6 g
Cholesterol: .... 77 mg
Sodium: .... 77 mg
Dietary Exchanges:.... 2 Starch
                             1 Vegetable
                             4 Lean Meat

❋ ❋ ❋

CHICKEN TETRAZZINI AMANDINE

1 Tbsp. + 1 tsp. reduced-calorie tub margarine
1-1/2 cups thinly sliced mushrooms
2 Tbsp. all-purpose flour
1-1/2 cups evaporated skimmed milk
1/2 cup low-sodium chicken broth
1 oz. toasted slivered almonds
1/2 tsp. dried basil
6-3/4 oz. Pasta Growers spaghetti, cooked and draine
8 oz. cubed cooked chicken breast
1 Tbsp. grated Parmesan cheese

Preheat oven to 350° F. Spray an 11x7" baking pan with nonstick cooking spray.

To prepare mushroom sauce, in small saucepan, melt margarine; add mushrooms. Cook, stirring frequently, 2 minutes Stir in flour; cook 1 minute, stirring constantly. Pour in 1/ cup of the milk, the broth and 1/2 cup water. Stir unt blended. Cook 2 to 3 minutes, stirring, until thickened. Re move from heat; stir in remaining 1 cup milk, the almond and basil.

Place spaghetti in prepared pan; top with chicken. Pou mushroom sauce over chicken; sprinkle with cheese.

Bake 20 to 25 minutes, until lightly browned and bubbly Let cool 5 minutes before serving.

Yield:	6 servings
Calories:	295
Fat:	7 g
Cholesterol:	35 mg
Sodium:	151 mg
Dietary Exchanges:	1-1/2 Breads, 1/2 Vegetable
	1-1/2 Meat, 1/2 Milk, 3/4 Fa

CHICKEN WITH FRESH ORANGE SAUCE

6 (3 oz.) boneless, skinless chicken breast halves
1/4 tsp. lemon pepper seasoning
Sauce:
1 Tbsp. sugar
1 tsp. cornstarch
1/4 tsp. very low-sodium chicken-flavor instant bouillon
1/4 tsp. grated orange peel
1/4 cup fresh orange juice
1/4 cup water

Spray broiler pan with nonstick cooking spray. Place chicken on spray-coated pan; sprinkle one side lightly with lemon pepper seasoning. Broil 4 to 6 inches from heat for 10 to 15 minutes or until chicken is fork tender and juices run clear, turning once.

Meanwhile, in small saucepan combine sugar, cornstarch, bouillon and orange peel; mix well. Stir in orange juice and water. Cook over medium heat until sauce comes to a boil and thickens slightly, stirring constantly. Serve sauce over chicken. If desired, garnish with orange slices.

Grill Directions: Heat grill. Sprinkle one side of chicken lightly with lemon pepper seasoning. Place chicken on gas grill over medium heat or on charcoal grill 4 to 6 inches from medium coals. Cook 10 to 15 minutes or until chicken is fork tender and juices run clear, turning once. Prepare sauce and serve as directed above.

TIP: To prepare sauce in microwave, combine sugar, cornstarch, bouillon and orange peel in 1-cup microwave-safe measuring cup. Stir in orange juice and water. Microwave on HIGH for 1 to 2 minutes or until sauce comes to a full boil and thickens slightly.

Yield:	6 servings
Calories:	120
Fat:	2 g
Cholesterol:	53 mg
Sodium:	70 mg
Dietary Exchanges:	2 Lean Meat

FRENCH GLAZED CHICKEN

1 lb. skinless, boneless chicken breasts
1/4 cup low calorie French dressing
2 Tbsp. low sugar apricot jam
1 Tbsp. dried onion
2 Tbsp. water

Arrange chicken in a 9x9 inch pan that has been sprayed with non-stick coating. Follow directions below for microwave or conventional oven.

Conventional Oven: Preheat oven to 350° F. Bake uncovered, for 20 minutes. Mix remaining ingredients and spoon over chicken. Return to oven for 10 minutes or until chicken is done and glaze is heated.

Microwave Method: Cover with plastic wrap, venting one corner. Cook on high for 6 to 8 minutes depending on thickness of chicken. Rotate 1/4 turn halfway through cooking. Drain any liquid. Mix remaining ingredients and spoon over chicken. Cook for 1 to 2 minutes or until glaze is heated.

Yield: .... 4 servings
Calories: 190
Fat: .... 4 g
Cholesterol: .... 78 mg
Sodium: .... 206 mg
Dietary Exchanges:.... 1 Vegetable
.... 4 Lean Meat

*Due to the low fat content of chicken breasts, the calories are less than the exchanges would compute

HOT CHICKEN POCKETS

3/4 cup plain low-fat yogurt
1/2 cucumber, peeled and seeded
1/2 tsp. dill weed
2 whole chicken breasts, boned and skinned
1-1/2 Tbsp. vegetable oil
1/4 tsp. garlic powder
6 pocket breads
6 radishes, thinly sliced
2 green onions, thinly sliced

In blender or food processor, combine yogurt, cucumber and dill weed. Blend until smooth. Set aside.

Slice chicken breasts across the muscle 1/4" thick. Slice these into 1/4" wide matchsticks.

In a heavy skillet, heat the oil. Add the garlic powder and chicken strips. Cook and stir over high heat until no pink remains.

Cut pockets in half. Fill with chicken, radishes and onion. Top with sauce and serve immediately.

Yield: .... 12 (1/2 pocket) servings
Calories: 181
Fat: .... 6.9 g
Cholesterol: .... 32 mg
Sodium: .... 40 mg
Dietary Exchanges:.... 1 Starch
.... 2 Lean Meat

ITALIAN GRILLED CHICKEN

1 lb. skinless chicken pieces
1/2 cup reduced-calorie Italian dressing

Marinate the chicken pieces in the reduced-calorie Italian dressing for 20 minutes, then broil.

Yield: .... 4 servings
Calories: 169
Fat: .... 6 g
Cholesterol: .... 69 mg
Sodium: .... 297 mg
Dietary Exchanges:.... 3 Lean Meat

SUPERFAST RECIPE

ITALIAN STEAMED CHICKEN

3 lbs. skinned chicken pieces
8 oz. no added salt tomato sauce
1/2 tsp. garlic powder
1 tsp. oregano
1 tsp. basil
1 tsp. sugar
1 tsp. lemon juice

Place skinned chicken pieces in microwave casserole dish. Mix no added salt tomato sauce with garlic powder, oregano, basil, sugar and lemon juice. Pour sauce over chicken and cover. Microwave at 70% power for 16 to 18 minutes.

Yield:	4 servings
Calories:	163
Fat:	4 g
Cholesterol:	67 mg
Sodium:	73 mg
Dietary Exchanges:	3 Lean Meat

SUPERFAST RECIPE

❊ ❊ ❊

LIGHT SOUR CREAM CHICKEN ENCHILADAS

1 (8 oz.) container light sour cream
1 (8 oz.) container nonfat plain yogurt
1 (10-3/4 oz.) can cream of chicken soup
  with 1/3 less salt
1 (4 oz.) can diced green chilies
12 (6-7 inch) white corn or flour tortillas
4 oz. (1 cup) shredded reduced-fat Cheddar chees(
1-1/2 cups chopped cooked chicken
1/4 cup sliced green onions

Heat oven to 350° F. Spray 13x9 inch (3 qt.) bakin;
dish with nonstick cooking spray. In med. bowl, com
bine sour cream, yogurt, soup and chilies; mix well
Spoon about 3 Tbsp. sour cream mixture down center o
each tortilla. Reserve 1/4 cup cheese; sprinkle each tor
tilla with remaining cheese, chicken and onions. Roll up
place in spray-coated dish. Spoon remaining sour cream
mixture over tortillas. Cover with foil.

Bake for 25 to 30 minutes or until hot and bubbly
Remove foil; sprinkle with reserved 1/4 cup cheese. Re
turn to oven; bake uncovered an additional 5 minute:
or until cheese is melted. Garnish with shredded lettuc(
and chopped tomatoes, if desired.

Yield:	6 servings
Calories:	380
Fat:	12 g
Cholesterol:	55 mg
Sodium:.........................	850 mg
Dietary Exchanges:	3 Starch
	2 Lean Meat
	1 Fat

LIME-HONEY-GLAZED CHICKEN

2 tsp. cinnamon
1 (3 lb.) chicken, cut up
1/2 cup honey
1/2 cup dry sherry
2 Tbsp. fresh lime juice
1 garlic clove, finely chopped
1/4 tsp. freshly ground pepper

Sprinkle cinnamon over chicken and arrange in 12x8x2 inch baking dish. Combine remaining ingredients in small bowl. Pour over chicken pieces and cover and marinate in refrigerator at least 3 hours, turning pieces occasionally. Bake at 350° F for 50 minutes, basting frequently with pan juices.

Yield: .... 6 servings
Calories: 504
Fat: .... 10 g
Cholesterol: .... 191 mg
Sodium: .... 178 mg
Dietary Exchanges:.... 2 Fruit
4 Lean Meats

Karen Stensrud
Dakota Medical Center

MASHED POTATO SHELL TACO PIE

1/4 cup liquid butter substitute
(for potatoes)
2/3 cup skim milk
1 (1-1/4 oz.) pkg. taco seasoning
mix
2-1/2 cups instant mashed potato
flakes
1/2 lb. ground white meat,
skinless turkey
1/2 cup chopped onion
2 cups refried beans (recipe to
follow) or 2 cans fat-free refried
beans
1/2 cup Bar-B-Q sauce

Refried Beans:
2 cups (17 oz. can)
cooked or canned
pinto beans
1/2 cup fat-free chicken
broth
2 Tbsp. chili powder
2 to 3 tsp. cumin
1/2 tsp. lite salt
(optional)
1/8 tsp. pepper
1/2 cup chopped cooked
onions
1/2 cup salsa

1 cup shredded lettuce
1 med. tomato, chopped
1 cup grated non-fat Cheddar cheese

Refried Beans: Over medium heat, in a non-stick skillet, combine beans and fat-free chicken broth, stirring occasionally (about 5 minutes). Mash beans; stir in chili powder, cumin, salt and pepper. Add more liquid to the skillet if necessary. Add onions and salsa. Cook and stir until a smooth paste forms.

In a medium saucepan combine liquid butter substitute, milk and 2 Tbsp. of the taco seasoning mix. Remove from heat; stir in potato flakes. Press mixture over the bottom and up the sides of a 10-inch quiche dish or pie plate that has been sprayed with a non-fat cooking spray. Microwave ground turkey and chopped onion covered with waxed paper for about 5 minutes on high. Stir after 2 minutes. Drain mixture in a colander to remove any fat. Place the turkey mixture in a large non-stick skillet. Stir in remaining seasoning mix, refried beans, and Bar-B-Q sauce. Cook until bubbly. Pour into prepared potato crust. Bake, uncovered, in a 350° F oven for 30 to 35 minutes. Let stand 5 minutes. Cut into 6 wedges and top each wedge with lettuce, tomatoes and grated cheese. You can also serve taco or hot sauce on the side.

Yield: .... 8 servings
Calories: 214
Fat: .... 1.8 g
Cholesterol: .... 19 mg
Sodium: .... 652 mg
Dietary Exchanges: .... 2 Breads, 1 Vegetable, 1 Meat

MEXICAN STYLE CHICKEN AND RICE

1 med. onion, chopped
1 green pepper, chopped
1 tsp. minced garlic
1 can (16 oz.) canned tomatoes*
1 can (4 oz.) chopped chilies
1 can (14-1/2 oz.) chicken broth
   (30% less salt), fat removed
1-3/4 cups quick cooking brown rice
6 drops Tabasco sauce
2 lbs. boneless, skinless chicken breasts
2 oz. grated, low fat cheddar cheese

Preheat oven to 350° F. Cook onion and pepper in a skillet that has been sprayed with non-stick coating. Add next six ingredients. Mix well and bring to a boil. Remove from heat and spoon into a 12x9 inch baking pan that has been sprayed with non-stick coating. Arrange chicken on top of rice mixture. Bake, covered, for 35 minutes or until rice is done. Sprinkle cheese over chicken. Let stand, 5 minutes or until cheese is melted.

Yield:	8 servings
Calories:	285
Fat:	5 g
Cholesterol:	78 mg
Sodium:	274 mg
Dietary Exchanges:	1 Starch
	1 Vegetable
	4 Lean Meat

*Sodium is figured for canned without salt.

**Due to the low fat content of chicken breasts, the calories are less than the exchanges would compute.

MOCK SAUSAGE PATTIES

1 lb. ground turkey (or chicken)
1/4 cup salt-free seasoned bread crumbs
2 Tbsp. low-sodium chicken broth
2 Tbsp. minced onion
1 Tbsp. minced fresh parsley
1 tsp. canola oil
1/4 tsp. ground sage
1/4 tsp. ground thyme
1/8 tsp. ground black pepper
1 lg. egg white

In medium-size bowl, combine all ingredients, except egg white. Using hands, blend ingredients well. Gently beat egg white with a fork; add to mixture and incorporate with hands or large wooden spoon. Shape into 12 patties. Place on non-stick cookie sheet (or cover regular cookie sheet with aluminum foil and spray with non-stick vegetable spray). Broil 3 to 4 inches from heat source 4 to 5 minutes or until light brown. Turn and broil additional 2 to 3 minutes, or until cooked through.

Yield:	6 servings
Calories:	161
Fat:	8.71 g
Cholesterol:	51.24 mg
Sodium:	87 mg
Dietary Exchanges:....	2 Lean Meats
	1-1/2 Fat

Rita Stutzinger
Dakota Medical Center

SAUSAGE AND SAUERKRAUT

1 jar (32 oz.) sauerkraut
1 lb. turkey smoked sausage
2 cups unpeeled potatoes, thinly sliced
1/2 cup onion, thinly sliced

Convention Oven: Preheat oven to 350° F. Drain sauerkraut. Add water and drain. Add water and drain again. Place in a large casserole. Top with onions and potatoes. Cut sausage into serving pieces (about 10) and place on top. Cover and cook for 1 hour or until potatoes are tender.

Microwave Method: Cook potatoes and onions on high for 5 minutes, stirring once halfway through cooking time. Drain sauerkraut. Add water and drain. Add water and drain again. Top potatoes with sauerkraut. Cut sausage into serving size pieces (about 10). Place over sauerkraut. Cover and microwave on high for 7 minutes, rearranging halfway through cooking time.

Yield:	5 servings
Calories:	210
Fat:	6 g
Cholesterol:	48 mg
Sodium:	1206 mg
Dietary Exchanges:	1 Starch
	1 Vegetable
	2 Lean Meat

Variation: Substitute shredded cabbage for all or part of the sauerkraut. Cook with potatoes, before adding sausage, when using the microwave.

The sodium from the sauerkraut is significantly reduced by rinsing it twice, however, it can be reduced further by substituting cabbage. This recipe is still high in sodium, due to the sausage, and should be limited.

SKILLET GOULASH

1 lb. fresh lean ground turkey
1 (16 oz.) pkg. frozen broccoli, roletti pasta,
    corn and carrots with garlic seasoning
1 (14.5 oz.) can no-salt-added whole tomatoes
    undrained, cut up
1 (10-3/4 oz.) can condensed 99%-fat-free
    tomato soup with 1/3 less salt
1/8 tsp. pepper

In large skillet, cook ground turkey until no longe
pink; drain. Stir in remaining ingredients. Bring t
a boil. Reduce heat; cover and simmer 3 to 5 min
utes or until thoroughly heated, stirring occasion
ally.

Yield: .... 5 (1-1/4 cup) servings
Calories: 320
Fat: .... 12 g
Cholesterol: .... 66 mg
Sodium: .... 620 mg
Dietary Exchanges:.... 1 Starch
                        3 Vegetable
                        2-1/2 Lean Meat
                        1 Fat

✳ ✳ ✳

SWEET AND SOUR CHICKEN

1 can (8 oz.) unsweetened pineapple chunks,
    packed in juice
1 lb. boneless, skinless chicken breasts
1 cup chicken broth (30% less salt)
1/4 cup vinegar
1/4 cup brown sugar or artificial sweetener*
2 tsp. soy sauce
1/2 tsp. chopped garlic
1 cup sliced celery
1 sm. onion, quartered
1 green pepper, sliced
3 Tbsp. cornstarch
1/4 cup water

Drain pineapple, reserving the juice. Cut chicken into bite size pieces and place in a saucepan. Add reserved juice, broth, vinegar, brown sugar, soy sauce, and garlic. Cover and simmer over low heat for 15 minutes. Add vegetables and pineapple. Cook 10 minutes, stirring occasionally. Combine cornstarch and water. Gradually stir into hot mixture. Continue o cook until thickened, stirring constantly. Serve with quick cooking brown rice.

Yield:	5 (1 cup) servings
Calories:	230 with sugar
	190 with artificial sweetener
Fat:	2 g
Cholesterol:	62 mg
Sodium:	343 mg
Dietary Exchanges:	1 Starch w/Sugar, 1/2 Starch w/Artificial Sweetener
	1 Vegetable
	1/2 Fruit
	3 Lean Meat

*If using artificial sweetener, add 5-6 packets after mixture is thickened with cornstarch.
**Due to the low fat content of chicken breasts, the calories are less than the exchanges would compute.

STIR-FRY

1 lb. lean boneless chicken, beef, or pork,
  cut in 1/4" strips
1 Tbsp. vegetable oil
1 sm. onion, sliced in rounds
1 garlic clove, minced
1 lb. fresh broccoli, stems cut in
  1/8" diagonal rounds, florets separated
1/2 lb. carrots sliced in 1/8" diagonal rounds
1 Tbsp. sodium-reduced soy sauce
1/4 lb. mushrooms

In a wok or large skillet over high heat, quickly brown
meat strips in hot oil. Add onion, garlic, broccoli
stems and carrots. Cook and stir constantly until
vegetables are hot but crisp. Add broccoli florets and
soy sauce. Cook and stir 1 to 2 minutes.

Yield: .... 4 oz. serving size
Calories: 218
Fat: .... 5.43 g
Cholesterol: .... 65.3 mg
Sodium: .... 218 mg
Dietary Exchanges:.... 1 Vegetable
                        4 Lean Meat

Noreen Thomas, Nutritionist
Dakota Medical Center

STIR-FRY

1/2 lb. lean beef, pork, or chicken cut into
   1/4 inch strips or 1/2 lb. of scallops
   or shrimp
1 sm. onion, sliced
1 tsp. chopped garlic
2 cups fresh broccoli flowerets
1 cup sliced carrots
1 cup sliced mushrooms
1 tsp. soy sauce
2 to 4 Tbsp. water

Spray a skillet with non-stick coating. Add meat or seafood and stir-fry with garlic until cooked. Remove and keep warm. Stir-fry carrots and onion until carrots are partially done. Add water, as needed, to prevent sticking. Add broccoli, mushrooms, and soy sauce. Stir-fry until vegetables are done to your liking. Add meat or seafood. Serve with rice or noodles.

Other vegetables that are good in stir-fry are: green or red peppers, celery, green onions, zucchini, cauliflower, cabbage, snow peas, bean sprouts.

Yield:	4 servings			
	Beef	Pork	Chicken	Shrimp
Calories:	150	150	135	100
Fat:	3 g	5 g	2 g	Trace
Cholesterol:	35 mg	39 mg	38 mg	83 mg
Sodium:	160 mg	162 mg	166 mg	228 mg
Dietary Exchanges:	2 Veg.	2 Veg.	2 Veg.	2 Veg.
	2 lean meat	2 lean meat	2 lean meat	1 lean meat

Due to the low fat content of chicken, the calories are less than the exchanges would compute.

❄ ❄ ❄

SWEET STIR FRY

1 lb. chicken - skinless, boneless, cut up
4 oz. tomato sauce
3 Tbsp. cider vinegar
3 Tbsp. brown sugar
16 oz. pkg. stir fry vegetables
8 oz. pineapple chunks

Place water in heated wok or electric fry pan. Quickly brown the cut up chicken. Add vegetables. Add tomato sauce, cider vinegar, brown sugar, and juice from pineapple. Stir in pineapple chunks. Cook and stir constantly. Serve when chicken is thoroughly cooked and vegetables are crisp and not soggy/soft

Yield: .... 6 servings
Calories: 222
Fat: .... 3.58 g
Cholesterol: .... 63.7 mg
Sodium: .... 203 mg
Dietary Exchanges:.... 1 Vegetable
1 Fruit
2 Lean Meat

Noreen Thomas, Nutritionist
Dakota Medical Center

CHICKEN OR FISH FILLETS

1 lb. skinless, boneless chicken pieces
   or fish fillets
Skim milk
Bisquick
1/2 tsp. margarine for each piece
Lemon pepper or garlic powder or paprika

Pat 1 lb. of skinless, boneless chicken pieces or fish fillets dry. Roll in skim milk and baking mix, such as Bisquick. Place on baking sheet and dot each piece with 1/2 tsp. margarine. Season with lemon pepper or garlic powder or paprika. Bake fish for 20 to 25 minutes and chicken for 40 to 45 minutes at 400° F.

Yield: .... 4 servings
Calories: 191
Fat: .... 5 g
Cholesterol: .... 67 mg
Sodium: .... 232 mg
Dietary Exchanges:.... 1/2 Starch/Bread
                         3 Lean Meat

SUPERFAST RECIPE

CORNFLAKE CHICKEN OR FISH

2 egg whites, whipped
1-1/2 cups evaporated skim milk
1 tsp. poultry seasoning
3 cups crushed cornflakes
1 lb. chicken, skinned, in pieces
   or 1 lb. frozen fish fillets

Preheat oven to 400° F. Combine egg whites, milk and seasoning in a mixing bowl. Whip for 2 minutes. Meanwhile, crush cornflakes in a plastic bag. Dip chicken or fish in milk, then shake in cornflakes and place on a baking sheet. For chicken, bake for 35 to 45 minutes. For fish, reduce time to 15 to 20 minutes.

Yield: .... 4 (3 oz.) servings
Calories: 215
Fat: .... 9 g
Cholesterol: .... 66 mg
Sodium: .... 230 mg
Dietary Exchanges: .... 1/2 Bread/Starch
                        3 Lean Meat
Preparation Time: ...... 35 minutes for fish
                        55 minutes for chicken

CRAB DELIGHT

8 oz. imitation or fresh crab
1 pkg. (10 oz.) frozen Oriental Style vegetables
1/4 tsp. garlic powder
1/4 tsp. ground ginger
1 can (8 oz.) sliced water chestnuts, drained
2 tsp. soy sauce (Optional)

Combine crab, vegetables, and seasonings. Heat according to directions on package for cooking vegetables. Add soy sauce, water chestnuts and heat thoroughly.

Yield: .... 4 (1 cup) servings
Calories: 100
Fat: .... .5 g
Cholesterol: .... 11 mg
Sodium: .... 502 mg
Dietary Exchanges:.... 2 Vegetables
1 Lean Meat

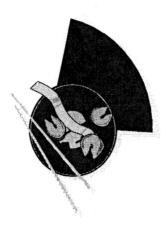

EASY SEAFOOD SALAD

1 cup salad shrimp, cooked
1 cup crab or flaked mock crab
1/2 cup chopped celery
1/4 cup chopped pimiento
2 Tbsp. minced onion
1 cup green peas, thawed
1/2 cup reduced-calorie 1000 Island dressing
1 tsp. lemon juice
1/4 tsp. pepper
1/4 tsp. marjoram
1/4 cup plain nonfat yogurt

Combine shrimp, crab, celery, pimiento, and onion in a serving bowl. In shaker container, mix salad dressing, lemon juice, pepper, marjoram, and yogurt. Pour dressing over salad, toss, and serve.

Yield: .... 4 (1 cup servings)
Calories: 154
Fat: .... 4 g
Cholesterol: .... 63 mg
Sodium: .... 388 mg
Dietary Exchanges:.... 1 Bread/Starch
                          1-1/2 Lean meat
Preparation Time: ...... 15 minutes

FISH IN FOIL

1 12-inch square of foil
4 oz. portion of flounder
Herbs and vegetables of your choice
1 tsp. sunflower margarine

You may use thinly sliced or julienned vegetables of your choice or 1/2 cup frozen mixed vegetables.

To prepare each packet, place fish in center of foil and sprinkle with one of the suggested combinations of ingredients. Fold foil over ingredients and secure all edges for a tight seal. Place in a shallow baking pan and bake in 375° F oven for 20 to 25 minutes or until fish turns opaque.

Suggested Combinations:
-Fish, Spinach, Lemon Juice, Nutmeg, Margarine
-Fish, Tomato (thinly sliced circles), Scallions (thin slices), Basil, Lemon Juice, Margarine
-Fish, Cucumber (thinly sliced circles), Lemon Juice, Dill, Parsley (chopped), Margarine
-Fish, Celery (thin slices), Lemon Juice, Thyme, Margarine
-Fish, Scallion Slices, Carrots (julienned), Curry Powder, Pepper, Margarine

Yield: .... 4 oz. servings
Calories: 173
Fat: .... 3.32 g
Cholesterol: .... 54.4 mg
Sodium: .... 169 mg
Dietary Exchanges: .... 1 Vegetable
                                       4 Lean Meat

FISH IN SALSA

1 lb. fish fillets (snapper, sole)
3/4 cup salsa

Arrange fish in a 9x13 inch pan that has been sprayed with non-stick coating. Follow directions below for microwave or conventional oven.

Conventional Oven: Preheat oven to 450° F. Bake uncovered, for 4 to 6 minutes per 1/2 inch thickness. Drain any liquid. Spoon salsa over fish. Return to oven for 2 minutes to heat salsa.

Microwave Method: Cover with plastic wrap, venting one corner. Cook on high for 4 to 6 minutes depending on thickness of fish. Rotate 1/4 turn halfway through cooking. Drain any liquid. Spoon salsa over fish. Cook for 1 to 2 minutes or until salsa is heated.

Yield:	4 (4 oz.) servings
Calories:	130
Fat:	1 g
Cholesterol:	40 mg
Sodium:	276 mg
Dietary Exchanges:....	1 Vegetable
	3 Lean Meat

*Due to the low fat content of fish, the calories are less than the exchanges would compute.

FRENCH GLAZED FISH

1 lb. fish fillets (snapper, sole)
1/4 cup low calorie French dressing
2 Tbsp. low sugar apricot jam
1 Tbsp. minced dried onion
2 Tbsp. water

rrange fish in a 9x13 inch baking pan that has een sprayed with non-stick coating. Follow directions for microwave or conventional oven below.

Conventional Oven: Preheat oven to 450° F. Bake, ncovered, for 4 to 5 minutes per half inch thickess of fish. Drain any liquid. Combine remaining ngredients and spoon over fish. Return to oven for minutes to heat sauce.

Microwave Method: Cover with plastic wrap, venting one corner. Cook on high for 4 to 6 minutes, epending on thickness of fish. Rotate 1/4 turn alfway through cooking time. Drain any liquid. Mix emaining ingredients and spoon over fish. Cook for to 2 minutes or until sauce is heated.

ield:	4 (4 oz.) servings
alories:	150
at:	2 g
holesterol:	41 mg
odium:	187 mg
ietary Exchanges:....	1/2 Fruit
	3 Lean Meat

Due to the low fat content of fish, the calories are ess than the exchanges would compute.

MICROWAVED SOLE WITH LEMON HERB SAUCE

1 cup julienne-cut (2x1/4x1/4 inch) carrots
2 Tbsp. water
1 lb. (1/2 inch thick) sole or flounder fillets,
    cut into 4 pieces
2 green onions, cut into 2-inch-long strips
1 Tbsp. margarine, melted
1 Tbsp. lemon juice
1 tsp. chopped fresh dill or 1/4 tsp. dried dill weed
1/4 tsp. salt

Microwave Directions: Place carrots and water in 1 qt. micro wave-safe casserole; cover. Microwave on high for 3 to 4 minutes or until carrots are almost crisp-tender; drain. Place fish fillets in 12x8 inch (2 qt.) or 8 inch square (1-1/2 qt.) microwave-safe dish. Arrange carrots and onions over fish.

In small bowl, combine margarine and lemon juice; drizzle over fish and vegetables. Sprinkle with dill. Cover with microwave safe plastic wrap. Microwave on high for 5 to 8 minutes or until fish flakes easily with fork, rotating dish 1/4 turn halfway through cooking. Sprinkle with salt.

Conventional Directions: Heat oven to 350° F. In small sauce pan, bring carrots and 1/4 cup water to a boil. Reduce heat to low; simmer 3 to 4 minutes or until carrots are almost crisp tender; drain. Place fish in ungreased 12x8 inch (2 qt.) or 8 inch square (1-1/2 qt.) baking dish. Arrange carrots and onions over fish.

In small bowl, combine margarine and lemon juice; drizzle over fish and vegetables. Sprinkle with dill. Cover with foil. Bake for 20 to 25 minutes or until fish flakes easily with fork. Sprinkle fish with salt.

Yield:	4 (4 oz.) servings
Calories:	150
Fat:	4 g
Cholesterol:	60 mg
Sodium:	270 mg
Dietary Exchanges:............	3 Lean Meat

MISTER TUNA PITA POCKETS

1 (6-1/8 oz.) can water-packed tuna,
   drained, flaked
1 (8 oz.) can crushed pineapple, well drained
1/4 cup shredded carrot
3 Tbsp. reduced-calorie mayonnaise
3 (6 inch) whole wheat or white pocket
   (pita) breads
Leaf lettuce, if desired

n small bowl, combine tuna, pineapple, carrot and
nayonnaise; mix well. Cut pocket breads in half
rosswise. Place lettuce in each pocket bread half;
ill each with 1/4 cup tuna mixture.

Yield: .... 6 (1 sandwich) servings
Calories: 170
Fat: .... 2 g
Cholesterol: .... 7 mg
Sodium: .... 360 mg
Dietary Exchanges:.... 1 Starch
                          1/2 Fruit
                          1 Lean Meat

ROUGHY ALMONDINE

4 orange roughy fillets
1 egg white
1/4 cup plain low-fat yogurt
1/4 cup toasted sliced almonds
1 to 2 tsp. grated orange rind

Poach fillets 4 minutes in simmering water. Drain
and dry thoroughly on paper toweling.

Whip egg white until stiff. Fold in yogurt, almonds
and orange rind. Coat the drained fillets with egg
white mixture.

Broil until brown and puffy (about 2 to 3 minutes)

Yield: .... 4 servings
Calories: 136
Fat: .... 5.7 g
Cholesterol: .... 52 mg
Sodium: .... 108 mg
Dietary Exchanges:.... 2 Lean Meat
                          1/2 Skim Milk

SALMON CAKES

1 can (15-1/2 oz.) red salmon, drained
(or 2 cups flaked)
1 tsp. onion powder
1/4 cup diced red pepper or canned pimiento
(2 oz. jar)
6 saltines (unsalted top), crushed
3 Tbsp. light salad dressing or mayonnaise
1 tsp. lemon juice
4 drops Tabasco

Remove skin from fish. Combine all ingredients in a medium bowl, mashing salmon bones with a fork. Shape into 4 cakes. Spray a skillet with non-stick cooking spray, and heat over medium heat. Cook salmon cakes, turning once, until lightly browned on each side.

Yield: .... 4 servings
Calories: 250
Fat: .... 14 g
Cholesterol: .... 73 mg
Sodium: .... 628 mg
Dietary Exchanges:.... 1/3 Starch
3 Medium-Fat Meat

SALMON LOAF

2 cups salmon and liquid
1 egg or 1/4 cup egg substitute
1 cup grated processed Cheddar cheese (lowfat
1 cup soft bread crumbs
1/2 tsp. salt
1/8 tsp. pepper
1 Tbsp. grated onion
1 Tbsp. melted margarine or canola oil

Preheat oven to 350° F. Mix together and bake fo
45 to 60 minutes in covered buttered casserole. Plac
in pan of water while baking.

Yield: .... 6 servings
Calories: 218
Fat: .... 9.16 g
Cholesterol: .... 43.25 mg
Sodium: .... 923 mg
Dietary Exchanges:.... 1 Bread
                        2 Lean Meat

Nutrition Alert: This recipe is high in sodium. Omi
salt and discard salmon liquid to reduce sodium.

SHRIMP CREAM TURNOVERS

    1 (8 oz.) ctn. (tub) light pasteurized process
        cream cheese product
    1 (6 oz.) pkg. frozen cooked tiny shrimp, thawed
    3 Tbsp. chopped fresh chives
    1/2 tsp. dried dill weed
    1/2 tsp. lemon pepper seasoning
    10 lg. (2 oz.) frozen white dough dinner rolls,
        thawed to room temperature

Grease 2 cookie sheets. In medium bowl, combine cream cheese product, shrimp, chives, dill and lemon pepper seasoning; mix well.

Roll or pat each dough roll into a 5 inch circle. Spoon 2 Tbsp. filling onto half of each circle, fold over to form half circles. Press rounded edges together securely with fork. Place 2 inches apart on greased cookie sheets; prick tops twice with fork. Cover with plastic wrap sprayed with nonstick cooking spray and cloth towel. Let rise in warm place (80 to 85° F) about 30 minutes or until doubled in size.*

Heat oven to 350° F. Uncover dough; bake 15 to 20 minutes or until golden brown. Cool slightly before serving.**

TIPS: *To decrease rise time, heat oven to 200° F. TURN OVEN OFF. Cover rolls as directed; set in warm oven for 10 minutes or until doubled in size. Bake as directed above.

**Turnovers can be made ahead. Bake, cool completely, wrap and store in refrigerator. Unwrap; reheat on cookie sheet at 400° F for 10 minutes or until thoroughly heated.

Yield:	10 (1 turnover) servings
Calories:	220
Fat:	7 g
Cholesterol:	44 mg
Sodium:	470 mg
Dietary Exchanges:	2 Starch
	1/2 Lean Meat
	1 Fat

SPANISH BAKED FISH

   1 lb. fish fillets (snapper or sole)
   1 can (8 oz.) tomato sauce*
   1/2 tsp. chopped garlic
   1/2 cup sliced onions
   1/2 tsp. chili powder
   1/4 tsp. oregano
   1/4 tsp. cumin

Preheat oven to 450° F. Arrange fish in a baking
dish that has been sprayed with non-stick coating.
Mix remaining ingredients and pour over fish. Bake
for 10 to 20 minutes or until fish flakes easily.

Yield:	4 servings
Calories:	140
Fat:	1 g
Cholesterol:	42 mg
Sodium:	89 mg
Dietary Exchanges:....	1 Vegetable
	3 Lean Meat

*Sodium is figured for unsalted

**Due to the low fat content of fish, the calories are
lower than the exchanges would compute.

✳ ✳ ✳

SPICED CREOLE SHRIMP

*A lovely tomato and vegetable sauce
that does full justice to your shrimp.*

1 green pepper, chopped
3/4 cup celery, diced
1/2 cup onion, diced
1-1/2 cups canned tomatoes
1/2 cup water
Sugar substitute to equal 1/4 cup
1/4 cup lemon juice
1 tsp. salt
1/2 tsp. oregano
Pepper
1-1/2 lbs. cooked shrimp
1 Tbsp. cornstarch

Combine first 10 ingredients and simmer until vegetables are tender, about 7 to 10 minutes. Add shrimp, and cook 3 minutes more. Combine cornstarch with a little cold water, and stir in to thicken sauce.

Yield:	6 servings
Calories:	135
Fat:	1.42 g
Cholesterol:	221.13 mg
Sodium:	710 mg
Dietary Exchanges:	1 Vegetable
	1 Lean Meat

Nutrition Alert: This recipe is high in sodium. Omit salt and use salt free tomatoes to reduce sodium.

VEGETABLE COD BAKE

1 lb. frozen cod fillets
3 Tbsp. lemon juice
1/2 tsp. paprika
1/2 cup sliced fresh mushrooms
1/4 cup chopped tomato
1/4 cup chopped green pepper
1 Tbsp. chopped fresh parsley
Freshly ground pepper
Lemon wedges

Thaw cod fillets. Cut into 4 portions and place in non-stick sprayed baking dish. Sprinkle with lemon juice and paprika.

Combine mushrooms, tomato, green pepper, parsley and pepper. Spread over fish. Cover and bake in 350° F oven for 25 minutes. Serve with lemon wedges.

Yield:	4 servings
Calories:	100
Fat:	0.3 g
Cholesterol:	36 mg
Sodium:	175 mg
Dietary Exchanges:....	2 Lean Meat

Thirst Quenchers

BUBBLY APPLE-ORANGE REFRESHER

1 qt. (4 cups) apple juice
1 qt. (4 cups) orange juice
1 - 6 oz. can frozen lemonade concentrate,
   thawed
1 (1-liter) bottle (4-1/4 cups) lemon-lime
   carbonated beverage, chilled

In 4-quart nonmetal container, combine juices and lemonade concentrate; stir until well blended.* Refrigerate. Just before serving, slowly add carbonated beverage; stir gently to blend. Serve over ice in glasses; garnish as desired.

*TIP: A clean 5-quart ice cream bucket can be used as a container.

Yield: .... 25 (1/2 cup) servings
Calories: 70
Fat: .... 0 g
Cholesterol: .... 0 mg
Sodium: .... 10 mg
Dietary Exchanges: .... 1 Fruit

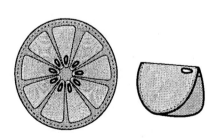

CRAN-APRICOT COOLER

> 1 (8-1/4 oz.) can unpeeled apricot halves
>   in real fruit juices, undrained
> 3/4 cup frozen cranberry cherry juice
>   concentrate (from a 12-oz. can)*
> 1 cup chilled mineral water

In blender container, combine all ingredients. Cover
blend until frothy and smooth. Serve immediately.

*TIP: Other frozen cranberry juice combinations
such as cranberry apple, cranberry orange or cranberry raspberry, can be substituted for cranberry
cherry juice concentrate.

Yield: .... 6 (1/2 cup servings)
Calories: 110
Fat: .... 0 g
Cholesterol: .... 0 mg
Sodium: .... 0 mg
Dietary Exchanges:.... 2 Fruit

CITRUS TEA

5 cups water
1/3 cup sugar
1/4 cup orange juice
2 Tbsp. lemon juice
4 spiced herbal tea bags
Lemon slices

In medium saucepan, combine water, sugar, orange juice and lemon juice. Bring to a boil. Remove from heat; add tea bags. Cover; let stand 10 minutes. Remove tea bags. Serve with lemon slices.

Yield: .... 5 (1 cup) servings
Calories: 60
Fat: .... 0 g
Cholesterol: .... 0 mg
Sodium: .... 0 mg
Dietary Exchanges:........ 1 Fruit

HOT CHOCOLATE MIX

1-1/3 cups nonfat dry milk
1/4 cup cocoa
4 packets sugar substitute
1 qt. boiling water
1 tsp. vanilla

Mix nonfat dry milk with cocoa and sugar substitute in a 1-1/2 quart heatproof container. Add the
boiling water and stir to mix. Stir in vanilla and serve
Preparation time: 5 minutes.

Yield: .... 4 (1 cup) servings
Calories: 100
Fat: .... 2 gm
Cholesterol: .... 7 mg
Sodium: .... 35 mg
Dietary Exchanges:.... 1 Skim Milk

HOT FRUITED TEA

5 cups boiling water
4 tea bags or 4 tsp. instant tea
10 whole cloves
1/4 tsp. cinnamon
2 Tbsp. sugar or to taste
3 Tbsp. lemon juice
1/3 cup orange juice
Orange slices or wedges

In large teapot, pour boiling water over tea, cloves and cinnamon. Cover; let steep 5 minutes. Strain tea; stir in sugar and juices. Heat to simmering. Serve hot with orange slice or wedge.

Diabetics use sugar substitute.

Yield:	11 (1/2 cup) servings
Calories:	13
Fat:	.02 g
Cholesterol:	0 mg
Sodium:	1 mg
Dietary Exchanges:	Free

Jan Sliper, LRD
Robyn Vinje, MS, LRD
Kathy Tehven, LRD
Paula Anderson, LRD
Lorraine Hanna, LRD
Dakota Medical Center

JOKER'S STRAWBERRY DAIQUIRI

1 (6 oz.) can frozen limeade, thawed
1-1/2 cups frozen unsweetened
    strawberries, partially thawed
1/3 cup powdered sugar
3-1/3 cups (28 oz.) lime or lemon-lime
    sparkling mineral water, chilled
1 to 2 tsp. rum extract
1 cup assorted chilled fresh fruit slices
    such as strawberries, limes, lemons,
    kiwifruit and/or star fruit

In food processor bowl with metal blade or blende
container, combine limeade, strawberries and pow
dered sugar. Process for 30 to 45 seconds or unti
pureed. Spoon mixture into large bowl or smal
punch bowl. Add mineral water and rum extract
mix well. Garnish with chilled fruit slices.

Yield: .... 6 (1/2 cup) servings
Calories: 110
Protein: .... 0 g
Carbohydrate: .... 29 g
Fat: .... 0 g
Cholesterol: .... 0 mg
Sodium: .... 30 mg
Dietary Exchanges:.... 2 Fruit

MIDNIGHT MALT

1 cup vanilla ice milk
1 cup 1% low-fat milk
2 Tbsp. chocolate malted milk powder
1/4 tsp. vanilla extract
1/8 tsp. ground cinnamon

Combine first 4 ingredients in container of an electric blender; cover and process until smooth. Pour into glasses and sprinkle with cinnamon. Serve immediately.

Yield: .... 2 (1 cup) servings
Calories: 180
Fat: .... 4 g
Cholesterol: .... 14 mg
Sodium: .... 153 mg
Dietary Exchanges:.... 1 Bread
                        1 Skim Milk

ORANGE JULIUS

6 oz. frozen orange juice concentrate
1 cup milk
1 cup water
3 Tbsp. sugar
1/2 to 1 full tray of ice cubes

Combine all ingredients in blender. Blend 40 seconds and enjoy! (Thinner consistency with fewer ice
cubes and thick enough to eat with spoon with full
tray of ice cubes.)

Yield: .... 4 (1/2 cup) servings
Calories: 123
Fat: .... .20 g
Cholesterol: .... 1.10 mg
Sodium: .... 32 mg
Dietary Exchanges:.... 2 Fruits

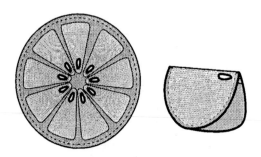

STRAWBERRY YOGURT SHAKE

1/2 cup unsweetened pineapple juice
3/4 cup plain low-fat yogurt
1-1/2 cups frozen, unsweetened strawberries
1 tsp. granulated sugar

Add ingredients, in order listed, to blender container.
Puree at medium speed, until thick and smooth.

Yield: .... 2 (1-1/2 cup) servings
Calories: 151
Fat: .... 2.09 g
Cholesterol: .... 5.60 mg
Sodium: .... 67 mg
Dietary Exchanges:.... 1 Fruit
                          1 Skim Milk

Rita Stutzinger
Dakota Medical Center

Rachel Rudel is a registered dietitian and writer.

She majored in Food and Nutrition and Education at North Dakota State University, Fargo, North Dakota. Over the years she has taught wellness classes, food safety, and consulted with school lunch programs in North Dakota and Minnesota. Rachel has been a feature writer for *The Forum* newspaper and multiple food and nutrition magazines. Presently, she is in clinical practice and is the co-editor and columnist for <u>*Diabetes 2002: Innovation, Vision and Balance for Healthy Living*</u>, a diabetes newsletter published by Dakota Clinic, Fargo, North Dakota.